Which
PRESIDENT
KILLED
a MAN?

Tantalizing Trivia and Fun Facts About Our Chief Executives and First Ladies

JAMES HUMES

Illustrations by William Bramhall

Contemporary Books

Chicago   New York   San Francisco   Lisbon   London   Madrid   Mexico City
Milan   New Delhi   San Juan   Seoul   Singapore   Sydney   Toronto

The *McGraw·Hill* Companies

Library of Congress Cataloging-in-Publication Data

Humes, James C.
 Which president killed a man? : tantalizing trivia and fun facts about our chief executives and first ladies / James Humes.
  p. cm.
  Includes index.
  ISBN 0-07-140223-3 (acid-free paper)
  1. Presidents—United States—History—Miscellanea. 2. Presidents—United States—Biography—Miscellanea. I. Title.

 E176.1 .H88 2002
 973'.09'9—dc21   2002071475

Cover illustration by Taxi/Getty Images
Interior design by Andrea Reider
Interior illustrations by William Bramhall

1 2 3 4 5 6 7 8 9 0 AGM/AGM 1 0 9 8 7 6 5 4 3 2

ISBN 0-07-140223-3

McGraw-Hill books are available at special quantity discounts to use as premiums and sales promotions, or for use in corporate training programs. For more information, please write to the Director of Special Sales, Professional Publishing, McGraw-Hill, Two Penn Plaza, New York, NY 10121-2298. Or contact your local bookstore.

This book is printed on acid-free paper.

To my brother Graham

CONTENTS

FOREWORD

I love history, especially White House history, and I thought I knew a lot about it since I've covered nine presidents—from John F. Kennedy to George W. Bush—and over the years I have regaled my family and even audiences with my eyewitness, intimate anecdotes about the White House. But after reading James Humes's encyclopedic book, *Which President Killed a Man?*, I realized how little I know and how much I enjoy learning more.

This book is a gold mine of fascinating information about our leaders of the past and their families. With the phenomenal research Humes has done, our knowledge of who we are as a nation and how we got here is greatly enhanced. I wish every family could have this book on its bookshelves—and certainly every school library. Besides, it's a great way to test the knowledge of your family and guests at parties during cold winter nights.

Humes was inspired to write this book of questions and answers about our presidents after touring the White House as a young boy. His parents bought him a paperback book of facts about the presidents. Now Humes has put together his own book, and it's crammed with interesting facts and anecdotes. Did you know, for example, that President Theodore Roosevelt was called the "Black Man's Buddy" for befriending African Americans and for being the first president to appoint them to federal positions? And did you know that on the day of his assassination,

Abraham Lincoln took his wife, Mary Todd, for a ride? Reaching out to hold his wife's hand, Lincoln said: "Dear, I have never felt so happy in my life." Mrs. Lincoln responded: "You said the same thing just before our boy Willie died."

These and many other great insights are included in this wonderful omnibus about those who once lived in the White House. It's fun to read and learn at the same time.

—Helen Thomas

PREFACE

 The seed for this book was planted more than half a century ago by a visit to the White House. It was the pilgrimage that so many families take in the spring to see their national capital amid the height of the cherry blossoms—then to be followed by a side trip from Washington, D.C., south to Williamsburg in Virginia. For Judge Sam Humes, his wife, Elenor, and their three sons, it was in 1941, the first year the restored Colonial Williamsburg was opened to the public. In our new powder blue Lincoln Zephyr, we drove from Williamsport, Pennsylvania, south on U.S. Route 15 to Washington.

We parked on Pennsylvania Avenue right in front of the White House. We then proceeded to follow the visitor's line through those first floors of the White House open for viewing. Upon leaving, we purchased a paperback fact book on the presidents with a picture of George Washington's face adorning the cover. That book, with its engravings of bearded countenances, reminded me of the two brothers of cough drop fame.

While our staunch Republican of a father attempted to see President Roosevelt on the strength of a letter from a mutual friend, my mother and the three of us boys waited for our father to emerge from the White House. My mother smoldered at the prospect of our father fraternizing with the enemy as my two older brothers started to fight in the backseat.

To quiet them, my mother took out the book on the presidents, giving it to my oldest brother, Sam, to divert him.

That presidential paperback would then later lie over the small desk-top radio in the old nursery next to our bedroom. The factoids in the book still leap into my memory six decades later: James Buchanan, bachelor president; Benjamin Harrison, grandson of a previous president; William Howard Taft, president and also chief justice; James Polk, president and former Speaker of the House; and particularly Grover Cleveland, who hanged three men!

In 1969, this presidential fact book would prompt me to assemble "the White House Quiz"—a one hundred–question test composed with the aid of fellow Nixon speechwriter Lee Huebner along with help from John McClaughry and Robin West one slow summer weekend. Other questions were added—not solely about presidents. "What foreign capital is named after a U.S. president?" "Name the four state capitals named after U.S. presidents." "What are the four commonwealths in the Union?" "What is the country in Europe that has a predominant religion other than Christianity?" "What states are the farthest northern, eastern, southern, and western in latitudes and longitudes?" "Name ten cities in the world with over a million population, beginning with the letter *M*." "Name the only vice president who resigned" (not knowing that the then-current vice president would resign four years later).

"The White House Quiz" had grades assigned to the respondents. The score of ninety qualified you as a summer Harvard intern. A score of ten—that of vice president! Interestingly, the highest score (except those of ourselves, who created the questions—but no one else knew that!) was Pat Moynihan's. Vice President Spiro Agnew's office called me for many of the answers because they heard I had scored the highest!

Some questions from that 1941 presidential fact book were sprung by my brother Graham on his grandson, Christopher Bartlo, on a visit to his daughter's home last summer. Christopher is in that prepubescent age when boys and girls soak up facts as if they are sponges. I remember my preteen years when I poured over baseball statistics and the girls I knew collected data on film stars.

My brother's grandson is a bright, inquisitive youth, and he gobbled up the presidential tidbits. The favorite question in our family was "Which president received a 1,235-pound cheese?" because our paternal grandmother's ancestor Israel Cole from Cheshire, Massachusetts, was the one who carted it to the White House for Thomas Jefferson. That visit of my brother Graham with Christopher inspired him to call me with this book idea. At first, I was cool to the suggestion, but I warmed up to it as I started to think of a title—*Which President Killed a Man?*—and the question format to make it less like a fact book. It was my brother Graham who suggested putting it into sections—like "Sports" and "Religion." I thank him for launching me on this fun project.

ACKNOWLEDGMENTS

Anyone who assembles such teasing trivia in presidential history will be much indebted to William A. DeGregorio's *The Complete Book of U.S. Presidents*. His is the best reference book. Also excellent is the *Presidential Fact Book* by Joseph Nathan Kane. Although this book of mine is not intended as a reference book, these two books should be in and on the shelves of any presidential scholar.

I also am indebted to some of the presidential libraries—the Richard Nixon Library and Birthplace in Yorba Linda, California; the Gerald R. Ford Library in Ann Arbor, Michigan; the Lyndon B. Johnson Library and Museum in Austin, Texas; the Ronald Reagan Presidential Library in Simi Valley, California; the Dwight D. Eisenhower Presidential Library in Abilene, Kansas; the Franklin D. Roosevelt Library and Museum in Hyde Park, New York; the John Fitzgerald Kennedy Library in Boston, Massachusetts; and the Theodore Roosevelt Association in Oyster Bay, New York.

These libraries and museums should be supported for their endeavors in helping to reach and teach new generations about our presidents and our American heritage.

I also want to thank those at the University of Southern Colorado—Dean Rex Fuller, Professor Dick Eisenbeis, Professor Lia Sissom, and the able manager, Carol Prichard Toponce.

In addition, thanks to Linda Graham, who read and typed my manuscript.

ADMINISTRATION MILESTONES

Which president signed the first Civil Rights legislation?

Civil Rights Milestone

Dwight D. Eisenhower, in 1960, signed an administration-backed bill that provided sanctions against obstructing the voting rights of blacks. Three years earlier, Eisenhower had dispatched troops to Arkansas to ensure the safety of black students attempting to enroll at a Little Rock high school.

Who was the first president to deliver the same address from the Oval Office in two languages?

Gracias, Señor Presidente

George W. Bush in March 2001 delivered the Saturday radio address first in English and then in Spanish.

Which president was the first to invite an African American to the White House?

Let's Do Lunch

Theodore Roosevelt invited Booker T. Washington, the African American educator, for lunch at the White House. The visit stirred an outcry in the South. "Pitchfork Ben" Tillman, a Democratic senator from South Carolina, was particularly furious, claiming that because of TR's actions it would be a long time before blacks "learn their place again."

Who was the first president to recognize the State of Israel?

Israel Recognized

Harry Truman. In 1948, Truman was the first head of a major country to recognize Israel. The recognition was opposed in Truman's own State Department. They thought it would antagonize the Arab world and that it was influenced by political considerations in a presidential election year. Secretary of State George C. Marshall told President Truman that because of this action against Marshall's recommendation, he would not vote for Truman in the November election.

Who was the only president to resign his office?

Resignation and Reflection

Richard Nixon resigned on August 9, 1974. The votes in the Democratic House of Representatives were more than enough for impeachment. Some political aides wanted Nixon to fight for acquittal in the Senate, where a two-thirds vote is required for conviction, but Nixon wanted to spare the nation the ordeal.

Nixon had won one of the greatest landslide victories for reelection in 1972. He resigned in ignominy. He said about this failure to address the Watergate incident: "I gave my enemies the sword for my destruction."

Who were the only two presidents to be impeached?

Disgrace and Dishonor?

Andrew Johnson and Bill Clinton were both impeached by the House of Representatives. They were both acquitted by the Senate (Johnson by only one vote in the two-thirds that is needed for conviction).

In Johnson's case, Congress was attacking his policies of Reconstruction. Clinton was beset with a flood of charges of misconduct, impropriety, and corruption. According to one presidential historian, William A. DeGregorio in *The Complete Book of U.S. Presidents*, the number of scandals of the Clinton administration was unprecedented. "Not since Warren Harding has the office of the president been so disgraced."

Who was the first president to recognize the Soviet Union?

Roosevelt and Russia

Franklin Delano Roosevelt, in 1933. Woodrow Wilson had broken off relations in 1917 when Vladimir Lenin became the nation's head after the Russian Revolution. Roosevelt accepted the credentials of Soviet Ambassador Max Litinov.

Which president had the lowest approval rating of any president in the twentieth century?

Harry in Hot Water

Harry Truman, in November 1951, according to the Gallup Poll, earned an approval rating at 22 percent. Nixon in July 1974, just before he resigned, was at 23 percent.

It's now generally forgotten, but in 1950 there was introduced in the House a bill of impeachment against Truman. Truman's attorney general, Howard McGrath, was indicted. Several high officials in the White House and Treasury were convicted for corruption. Truman's taking over

the steel mill (faced with a steel strike during the Korean War, he had seized mills to keep them operating), the war in Korea, and the firing of General Douglas MacArthur all contributed to his unpopularity. In 1952, the Republican Party's slogan for cleaning up the mess was "Corruption, Communism, and Korea."

Who was the first president to broadcast in a foreign language?

Mes Amis, Bonsoir

Franklin Delano Roosevelt. In November 1942, as American troops were poised to land in North Africa, Roosevelt delivered a speech in French. Vichy, France, Hitler's puppet French government, was in control of the

French colonial possessions in North Africa. The Americans were hoping to find little resistance. Roosevelt, with the years of French he learned at Groton, read the text prepared for him.

Which president signed a law forbidding "false malicious and scandalous writing" against his administration?

Gag Rule

John Adams in 1798 signed the controversial Alien and Sedition Act. The legislation was directed against the emerging Democrat-Republican Party led by Thomas Jefferson, which was pushing for America to take sides with revolutionary France against Britain.

Which president earmarked as public preserves acres of forests, mountains, lakes, and rivers equal to the whole eastern seaboard?

For Land's Sake!

Theodore Roosevelt. In 1908, by executive order, he set aside hundreds of thousands of square miles of land for public use. The ban of private speculators from these tracts outraged some quarters of the business community. TR was the first conservation president.

Which president was the father of the interstate highway system?

Ike's Interstate

Dwight D. Eisenhower, in 1955, signed the act beginning the interstate system. The idea first originated with him in 1919, when Major Eisenhower led a military convoy across America to the West Coast. The truck convoy followed what was then U.S. Route 30 for about 3,200 miles at an average of six miles an hour. He became convinced then that a better federal highway system was needed.

Who was the first president to receive a black head of state at the White House?

Haiti's Head

John Adams. He received President Toussaint of Haiti in 1798. His successor, Thomas Jefferson, discontinued the recognition of the first black nation.

AGE

Who was the youngest president in the White House?

"Not That Damned Cowboy in the White House?"

These were the words of Senator Mark Hanna when he heard the news that President William McKinley had been shot in Buffalo in September of 1901. Theodore Roosevelt was a little over forty-two years and ten months when he was sworn in. In March of that year, when the political boss of New York, Tom Platt, was asked whether he was going to attend the inauguration of President McKinley for his second term, Platt said: "No. I'm going to see Teddy Roosevelt take the veil." Roosevelt had resigned the governorship of New York to assume the vice presidency.

Which president was the youngest presidential candidate?

"Jack Be Nimble, Jack Be Quick"

John F. Kennedy was the youngest presidential nominee elected. He was 43 years and 236 days old when he was inaugurated as president on January 20, 1961 (279 days younger than Theodore Roosevelt had been when he took the oath when McKinley died). Kennedy's interest in politics began early. His mother Rose said, "My son was rocked to sleep to political lullabies." When Joseph Kennedy Jr. was killed in World War II, his younger brother John became the focus of his father's, Ambassador Joseph Kennedy's, ambitions.

Which president lived the longest after he left office?

Hoover Holds On

Herbert Hoover lived thirty-three years after he left the presidency. John Adams lived twenty-five years after he left the White House—dying in 1826. Martin Van Buren died twenty-one years after his service as president.

Which president lived the longest?

Ron the Nonagenarian

On February 6, 2002, Ronald Reagan celebrated his ninety-first birthday. (In November 1994 the former president announced he had Alzheimer's disease.) The next oldest was Herbert Hoover, who lived to be ninety years and seventy days and died in 1964. At that time, Hoover had exceeded John Adams, who died at ninety years and forty-five days.

Which president wrote a one-sentence will?

Terse Testator

Calvin Coolidge. The president of few words lived up to that reputation when he wrote a one-sentence will leaving all his estate to his wife, Grace.

Who was the oldest president?

Old Man Ron

Ronald Reagan was the oldest president in history. Reagan was just short of his seventy-eighth birthday, when he left the White House in 1989. Dwight Eisenhower, when he left office in 1961, was only seventy.

Which president fathered a child at age seventy?

Old Goat?

In 1860, former president John Tyler witnessed the birth of a daughter named Pearl. Pearl was the seventh child of his second wife, Julia Gardiner Tyler. Pearl would die in 1947, more than a century after her father became president.

THE ARTS

Which president won a Pulitzer Prize for his biography about a preceding president?

President Writes About a President

Herbert Hoover. His *Ordeal of Woodrow Wilson* was published in 1958. This bestselling book was sympathetic to the president he served in World War I but criticized Wilson for not compromising with the Senate on the League of Nations.

The college friend of which president became an author more famous than the president?

Pen Mightier than the President

Franklin Pierce. Pierce and his lifelong friend, Nathaniel Hawthorne, met at Bowdoin College in Maine in 1821.

As senator, Pierce urged Hawthorne's appointment by President James K. Polk to be collector of Salem, a sinecure that allowed the author to write *The Scarlet Letter*. Later, President Pierce made Hawthorne U.S. consul in Liverpool, England.

In the summer of 1868, Hawthorne took Pierce, who was suffering from a stomach ailment, probably cirrhosis of the liver, to Saranac Lake. Pierce died that October.

Which president was given a music lesson by the celebrated pianist Ignace Paderewski?

Practice Makes Perfect

Harry Truman. Twelve-year-old Truman was a piano student in Independence, Missouri. His teacher took him to see Ignace Paderewski, who was performing in Kansas City. Afterward, the teacher took Truman to meet Paderewski. The Polish concert pianist asked Truman to play a piece. Truman had to play the work three times before Paderewski was satisfied.

Four decades later, President Roosevelt sent his vice president to meet Paderewski, then the former prime minister of Poland, who had fled his conquered country and had arrived in New York.

"It is an honor to meet the vice president of the United States," said Paderewski.

"No," said Truman, "you met me before. I was the boy whom you had play a piece three times before you were satisfied."

Who is the only president to have been saluted by a classical symphony written in his honor?

Copland's Composition

Abraham Lincoln. Aaron Copland in 1942 composed a symphony to commemorate the martyred president; it was called "Lincoln Portrait."

Which president employed two Pulitzer Prize–winning authors as presidential speechwriters?

Presidential Pens

Franklin Delano Roosevelt. The writers were Robert Sherwood and Archibald MacLeish.

Sherwood had won his Pulitzer for *Abe Lincoln in Illinois*. Roosevelt later made him director of war information.

MacLeish was recognized for his poetry. He would later write a verse drama, *J.B.*, published in 1958. Roosevelt would appoint him librarian of Congress.

Which president painted a portrait of a British prime minister?

"They Don't Talk Back"

President Dwight D. Eisenhower painted a portrait of Winston Churchill, against the prime minister's advice.

Churchill, an accomplished artist whose paintings have been hung in the Louvre, told him, "I do not paint portraits of people, Ike—only trees and mountains—because they don't talk back." Eisenhower painted the portrait in 1954. It now hangs in the Walter Reed Hospital, where Eisenhower died.

Which president delivered his own collection of books to establish the Library of Congress?

The Jefferson Collection

Thomas Jefferson. When the British burned the Capitol in the War of 1812, they destroyed its collection of books. To replace them, Jefferson sold his 6,500-volume collection to the United States for $23,950. It took eleven wagons to transport Jefferson's books to Washington. Jefferson at the time was heavily in debt.

William Dean Howells was the author of **The Rise of Silas Lapham** *and founder of the* **Atlantic Monthly.** *He wrote a presidential campaign biography of which president?*

Lincoln Partisan

Abraham Lincoln. The twenty-two-year-old Ohio reporter William Dean Howells was an early supporter of Lincoln, and he volunteered to write a campaign biography. When the president was elected, he appointed Howells to be the American consul to Venice. It would be the journalist's first trip to Europe. Howells was known for his realism in fiction.

Which president could quote passages from Shakespeare and kept the Bard's tragedies on his desk in his office in the White House?

"Out, Out, Brief Candle . . ."

Abraham Lincoln. Lincoln, who had only three years' schooling, kept four books on his White House desk: the U.S. Constitution, a copy of the U.S. Statutes, the King James version of the Bible, and a collection of Shakespeare's tragedies.

Lincoln had first been introduced to Shakespeare by a New Salem character, Jack Kelso. To some, Kelso was a town drunk; but to others who would listen, such as Lincoln, he was a walking repository of Shakespeare's dramatic verse. Kelso whetted Lincoln's interest in Shakespeare. Lincoln especially loved the Bard's tragedies. His favorite was *Macbeth*.

A few days before his fateful trip to Ford's Theater, Lincoln was heard in the White House reciting aloud that haunting soliloquy by the Scottish king:

> Out, out, brief candle!
> Life's but a walking shadow, a poor player
> That struts and frets his hour upon the stage
> And then is heard no more. 'Tis a tale
> Told by an idiot, full of sound and fury,
> Signifying nothing.

Which president wrote the first scholarly history of the War of 1812?

Solon and Scholar

Theodore Roosevelt. While a member of the assembly in New York, Roosevelt found time to write *The Naval War*, still considered one of the best studies of that war. Later, under President McKinley, Roosevelt would serve as assistant secretary of the navy, where he would champion a bigger fleet.

Which president had Robert Frost recite one of his poems at his inauguration?

Frost on a Frosty Day

John F. Kennedy. The New England president had the New England poet, the eighty-seven-year-old Frost, read one of his poems. Frost selected "The Gift Outright."

On that blowy, snowy day, his pages blew away in the midst of the recitation but were recovered. One of the lines went:

The land was ours before we were the land's.
She was our land more than a hundred years
before we were her people.

Who was the only president to publish commercially a book of his poetry?

Poet President

John Quincy Adams. He published his poetry after he left the White House. Most of his verse was inspired by scenes of nature.

Which first lady first installed a piano in the White House?

Music in the Mansion

Abigail Adams. The first first lady to live in what would later be called the White House found the new mansion dank and dreary. A piano's music was needed to cheer it up. She had learned to play in her father's church in Weymouth, Massachusetts. The piano was placed in the East Room.

Which president won a Pulitzer Prize before he became president?

"More Courage and Less Profile"

John F. Kennedy. In 1955, while Kennedy was recovering from spinal surgery, he wrote *Profiles in Courage*. It was about principled politicians making unpopular votes—Senator Edmund Ross in the impeachment of Andrew Johnson and Senator Robert A. Taft in opposing the Nuremberg trials were among the politicians Kennedy chose.

While Kennedy conceived of the idea, some believe that Ted Sorensen, his chief Senate aide (and later his top White House speechwriter), penned the initial draft. It won the Pulitzer Prize in 1956.

When Kennedy ran for president three years later, Eleanor Roosevelt opposed his candidacy for the Democratic nomination saying she wished he had "more courage and less profile." It was a gibe at the handsome Kennedy for having ducked the Senate's censure vote on Joseph McCarthy. McCarthy was a friend of his brother Robert and was a god-father to one of Robert's children. The anti-Communist McCarthy was popular in Irish Catholic Massachusetts.

Which two presidents made the architectural designs for buildings on their estates?

Building Blueprints

Thomas Jefferson was one, of course. The multifaceted Jefferson is well known for his design of Monticello, his home near Charlottesville, Virginia.

Less well known is that Franklin Delano Roosevelt designed his little house and office on the Hyde Park estate, which he had planned to use when he left the White House.

Mark Twain urged this man to be the first president to write his memoirs. The book became a bestseller. Who was the president?

Final Words?

Ulysses S. Grant. Samuel Clemens (or Mark Twain) urged the general to write his autobiography. Clemens had admired the clear muscular prose in Grant's letters. Grant, dying of cancer, finished the book days before his death, when he could no longer speak. The first royalty check, which arrived after his death, was more than $200,000, the world record for royalties at the time. The autobiography eventually earned more than half a million dollars, which gave his wife an ample income until her death.

About which president have sixteen hundred books been written?

"Little Note nor Long Remember"

Abraham Lincoln. The Library of Congress some years ago numbered that many books that have been written about the martyred "great emancipator." Furthermore, his Gettysburg Address is the most memorized speech in the world.

Which president conversed with his wife in Mandarin Chinese?

Chinese Puzzle

Herbert Hoover. When Hoover and his wife wanted to communicate a message without others present understanding it, they would converse in Chinese to the puzzlement of their company. Hoover and his wife had learned the language of the educated Chinese in the early 1900s, when he was a mining engineer in China.

The children of two presidents have written murder mysteries about Washington D.C. Who are the two presidents?

Whodunit?

Franklin Delano Roosevelt and Harry Truman. Elliott Roosevelt makes his mother the protagonist. Margaret Truman Daniels picks various locations—such as the White House, the Capitol, and the Smithsonian—about which a plot is woven.

Neither of the two actually wrote the texts, although they did supervise the writing. Interestingly, Franklin Delano Roosevelt always wanted to write a mystery. *The President's Mystery Story*, published in 1935 by Farrar and Rinehart, poses this question by FDR: how can a man disappear with five million dollars in negotiable forms and not be traced? Various authors submitted their answers.

The inventor Samuel Morse painted a portrait of a president that hangs in the White House. Who is the president?

"What Hath [Morse] Wrought?"

James K. Polk. The upstate New York artist painted the Tennessee president in the early days of Polk's presidency. Morse, who gained his electrical ideas from the Frenchman André-Marie Ampère, developed the telegraph in 1844, the year of Polk's election to the White House.

Which president took the description or name of his administration from a chapter in Mark Twain's A Connecticut Yankee in King Arthur's Court?

New Deal

Franklin Delano Roosevelt. "New Deal" was the Twain phrase he chose. Roosevelt once said, "If people like my choice of oratorical style, it is largely due to my constant study of Mark Twain's works."

But FDR, who copied the use of initials (as his cousin TR did), was also influenced by Theodore Roosevelt's use of the phrase "Square Deal" as a catchword for his administration. In his acceptance speech for the Democratic nomination in 1932, Franklin Delano Roosevelt said, "I pledge you, I pledge myself to a new deal for the American people."

Which president has had two volumes of a biography written about him by his grandson?

Eisenhower at War

Dwight D. Eisenhower. Dwight David Eisenhower II, better known as David Eisenhower, is a professor at the University of Pennsylvania. His book *Eisenhower*, published by Random House, came out in 1986. It is a book on the general's war years. The book on his presidency is still in process.

David's father, General John Eisenhower, is a celebrated and recognized military historian who has written highly praised books on the Battle of the Bulge, the Mexican War, and World War I.

Which president relaxed at the White House by translating Dante's Inferno *from medieval Latin?*

Magna cum Laude

Calvin Coolidge. Coolidge is not popularly considered to have had intellectual pursuits. The man who had been a Latin student at Amherst, however, found escape at the White House by reading and translating Dante. Coolidge also wrote most of his own speeches, including his most profound on July 4, 1926, for the sesquicentennial. The oration, which Coolidge delivered in Philadelphia, Pennsylvania, traced the theological origins of the Declaration of Independence.

Daisy Miller, in the novel by the same name by Henry James, was a character based on a presidential daughter. Who was the president?

"Don't Let Poor Nellie Starve"

Ulysses S. Grant. Nellie Grant was his high-spending, loud-talking, and gallivanting daughter. Henry James liked to depict brash Americans in the company of more refined Europeans. Nellie married an Englishman and lived in London until their separation.

Which two presidents played the violin?

Two Virginian Violinists

Thomas Jefferson and John Tyler. Jefferson was quite accomplished as a violinist until he broke his arm in Paris.

John Tyler became quite skilled in playing the violin to entertain his guests at the White House and later at his plantation house, Sherwood Forest, near Richmond, Virginia.

Which president, as a hobby, wrote bawdy limericks?

Lewd Laughter

Woodrow Wilson. The former professor and university president liked to write and recite ribald rhymes. One started:

> There was a lady from Niger
> who liked to ride a tiger . . .

Wilson used to regale his audiences with such ditties at the White House as well as when he was courting the widow (later to be his wife)

Edith Bolling Galt. Wilson himself was the object of lewd laughter when the *Washington Star* reported: "The president spent most of his time entering Mrs. Galt." The typo for "entertaining" was replaced after the first edition.

Many presidents have invited musicians to play or even be guests at state dinners at the White House. Who was the first president to host a dinner in honor of a performer?

"The Royalty of Music"

Richard Nixon. In 1969, he hosted a dinner in honor of Edward "Duke" Ellington. Nixon presented a presidential medal to Ellington; its inscription read: "In the royalty of music no one stands taller or swings higher than the Duke."

The dinner followed an earlier honoring of the artist Andrew Wyeth, whose representational portraits and landscapes the critics disliked but Nixon liked. The attention triggered the building of a Wyeth museum at Chadds Ford, Pennsylvania, where the artist lived.

Which president authored fourteen books before he entered the White House?

Readin', Ritin', and Roosevelt?

Theodore Roosevelt. The prolific Roosevelt wrote histories, biographies, studies of nature, and citizenship primers on patriotism. He was also the most voracious reader of the presidents. His biographer, Edward Morris, estimated that he read more than ten thousand books, many each week and some in languages other than English. To French and German envoys, he would quote by memory excerpts from books by authors such as Voltaire or Goethe in their original language. He possessed a photographic memory. Said the noted American journalist William Allen White, "I have never known such a man as he and never shall again."

BIRTH AND
DEATH

Which two presidents died on the Fourth of July in the same year?

Two Signers Sign Off

On July 4, 1826, fifty years after the signing of the Declaration of Independence in Philadelphia, two signers—Thomas Jefferson and John Adams—political foes who became friends—died. Adams's last words were: "Jefferson survives," not knowing that the president who had defeated him in 1800 had died earlier that morning.

Many clergymen at the time interpreted the double death of the two presidents on the fiftieth anniversary as a sign of Divine Providence.

Which president was born on the Fourth of July?

"A Yankee Doodle Dandy"

When Calvin Coolidge was president he was often regaled with George M. Cohan's song "I'm a Yankee Doodle Dandy . . . born on the Fourth of July." Coolidge was born on Independence Day 1872 in Plymouth, Vermont.

Which president's tomb was broken into and plundered?

Lincoln Looting?

In 1876 a gang of thieves broke into Abraham Lincoln's tomb in Springfield, Illinois. Their plan was to steal the casket and demand $200,000 for its return.

They unknowingly imparted their intentions to an undercover Pinkerton detective. As soon as the conspirators broke into the tomb and were pulling out the casket, they were arrested.

One president, according to some historians, was born in Canada and not the United States and, therefore, was ineligible to be president. Who was the president?

Cheating Chester?

Chester Alan Arthur always claimed that he was born in North Fairfield, Vermont, although no birth certificate has ever been found to confirm it. His political foes and some historians believed he was born across the border in Canada. Of course, if he had been born in Canada, he would have been ineligible to be vice president or president. Vice President Arthur succeeded James A. Garfield when Garfield died of an assassin's bullet in 1881.

Which two presidents are buried in Arlington National Cemetery in Virginia?

Two Graves

Almost everyone knows that John F. Kennedy, a naval lieutenant commander in World War II, is buried at Arlington where there burns an eternal flame at his grave. People are less familiar with the fact that William Howard Taft, who served as secretary of war, is also buried there. Technically, any president who serves in the role of commander in chief can be buried there. The land at Arlington was confiscated from the estate of General Robert E. Lee during the Civil War.

Who is buried in Grant's tomb?

"Massa's in the Cold, Cold Ground?"

The answer to the age-old silly question is: no one! Grant is not "buried." "Buried" means "put under ground." Grant's tomb lies above the ground. When Grant died, his friends wanted a mausoleum like Napoleon's in Paris. The result was Grant's tomb. Grant told his son that he wanted his final resting place to be in New York, in the city where he received his army commission and that had befriended him.

The last president born in a log cabin was Lincoln. Who was the first?

Log Cabin to White House

Andrew Jackson was the first. He was also the first to be born in South Carolina—in the frontier region of the Waxhaws close to the border of North Carolina. In 1767 he was born the third child to Andrew and Elizabeth Hutchinson Jackson, immigrants from Ireland.

Lucy Mercer Rutherfurd, a longtime inamorata of a president, was with him at his death. Who was the president?

Lucy and Franklin

Franklin Delano Roosevelt died on April 12, 1945, in Warm Springs, Georgia. He was in the midst of having his portrait painted by Elizabeth Shumatov. With him was Lucy Mercer Rutherfurd, who had introduced the artist to Roosevelt. Rutherfurd and Shumatov, along with a photographer, had driven over from the Mercer family home in Savannah. It was Roosevelt's daughter, Anna, who had suggested to Mrs. Rutherfurd that a visit might cheer up the weary president after his taxing conference in Yalta with Churchill and Stalin. Mrs. Roosevelt did not know of Mrs. Rutherfurd's visit and was deeply hurt when she found out later.

Lucy had been social secretary to Mrs. Roosevelt when Roosevelt was assistant secretary of the navy in World War I. When Mrs. Roosevelt found love letters written between Rutherfurd and Roosevelt, she almost divorced him. Roosevelt, while president, continued to see Rutherfurd from time to time. The train he took to Hyde Park from Washington would stop at a railroad siding in New Jersey near the widowed Mrs. Rutherfurd's home.

Who was the first president to be born in the United States?

"Born in the U.S.A."

Martin Van Buren. All of the preceding presidents were born on what is now U.S. soil but as British subjects. The eighth president was born on December 5, 1782—after the surrender of General Cornwallis's army in Yorktown in 1781.

Who was the first president born in a hospital?

Not at Home

Jimmy Carter. James Earl Carter Jr. was born October 1, 1924, at the Wise Clinic in Plains, Georgia.

A president's wife let it be known that she did not want this future president to attend her husband's funeral. Who was the president told to stay home?

The Missing Virginian

Thomas Jefferson. As president, George Washington was hurt by the attacks of Jefferson's lieutenants on his character—particularly that he wanted to be king. Jefferson was forming the first political party—the forerunner of today's Democratic Party. Class envy was the theme used to arouse Jefferson's followers, the farmers and frontiersmen. Aides like William Duane and others whom Jefferson had appointed had spread their scurrilous attacks on Washington's regal airs. Jefferson was disingenuous when confronted by Washington. Their relationship became estranged. Washington then turned to Alexander Hamilton as his principal adviser. When General Washington died in December 1799, Mrs. Washington conveyed the message that she did not want the then vice president and fellow Virginian Jefferson to attend the services at Mount Vernon.

Which president was buried in a simple ninety-five-dollar casket?

Simple Soldier

Dwight D. Eisenhower. He gave instructions that he wanted the ordinary army casket that was used for those who died on the landings at Normandy and are buried nearby.

The casket now rests on a bier in the chapel at Abilene, Kansas, the home of the Eisenhower Museum and Library. Eisenhower, who was born in a railway shack in Denison, Texas, grew up in Abilene.

Which president had as his pallbearers Robert Lincoln, son of Abraham Lincoln; Civil War General Philip Sheridan; furniture and interior designer Louis Tiffany; and railroad mogul Cornelius Vanderbilt?

Chester's Cortege

Chester Alan Arthur died at his home at 123 Lexington Avenue in New York City on November 18, 1886. The list of pallbearers for the Episcopal Church of the Heavenly Rest on New York's tony Upper East Side in New York City reflected the attraction to fame, money, and elegance of this self-made lawyer and politician.

CURIOSITIES

Which president defended the British officer responsible for the killings during the Boston Massacre?

Lobsterback Lawyer

John Adams. Lawyer Adams was the defense counsel for Captain Thomas Preston. On March 5, 1770, an angry group of protestors led by Crispus Attucks, a black merchant marine sailor, rallied some Bostonians to protest against a group of armed British soldiers in Boston. The hated occupying British redcoats were called "lobsterbacks." The demonstrators waved sticks and tried to snatch the soldiers' rifles. The British fired, and killed three. Adams, in Anglophobic Boston, displayed great courage in representing Preston. No other Boston lawyer was willing, but Adams feared that Preston would be hanged by a vengeful Boston jury. Adams's defense won an acquittal of Preston.

Which president is credited for giving rise to the expression "OK"?

Old Kinderhook

Martin Van Buren. Van Buren was born in Kinderhook, New York. He became known by the nickname "Old Kinderhook," and the O.K. Club of New York City, a Democratic Party organization, was formed in honor of Van Buren. The Democrats' use of "OK" as their slogan won a permanent place in American slang to mean "all correct."

Who served as president for only a day?

Sleep In?

David Atchison. Atchison was a senator from Missouri (the Atchison Topeka and the Santa Fe Railroad was taken from his name). Atchison was elected president pro tempore of the Senate on Friday, March 2, 1849, upon the nomination of Senator Thomas Hart Benton, also of Missouri. Two days later, March 4, at noon was when, according to the Constitution at the time, the presidential administration of James Polk officially ended. Vice President George Dallas had already resigned his office on March 2. There was, therefore, no president or vice president. March 4 fell on a Sunday. Zachary Taylor, for religious reasons, however, would not take his oath on the Sabbath. Thus, Atchison technically succeeded to the presidency. Atchison spent the day in bed signing no legislature acts or executive orders. Taylor took his presidential oath on Monday.

At his death, Atchison's home state of Missouri erected a monument with this inscription:

> David Rice Atchison 1807–1886. President of the U.S. for one day,
> Lawyer, Statesman, and Jurist.

In one year, three men served as president. Who were they?

Three's a Crowd?

Martin Van Buren, William Henry Harrison, and John Tyler all served as president in 1841. The eighth U.S. president, Van Buren, completed his term on March 3, 1841. The next day the ninth president, William Henry Harrison, was inaugurated. Harrison died on April 4. Then Vice President John Tyler was sworn in as the tenth president.

Which president is depicted on the $100,000 bill?

Grand Old Name

Woodrow Wilson. It is perhaps apt that the president responsible for creating the Federal Reserve System in 1913 should have his picture on the highest denomination of money in circulation.

Which president regularly took a "skinny dip" in the waters behind the White House?

Caught with His Pants Down?

John Quincy Adams. The sixth president was accustomed to taking an early morning nude swim in the Potomac, whose backwaters edged up behind the White House. One morning an enterprising reporter, Anne Royal, took his clothes as a ransom in exchange for an interview. Adams was forced to oblige her.

Which president had a secret operation performed on him to remove a cancerous jaw?

No Pleasure Cruise

Grover Cleveland. In 1893, Cleveland was suffering from cancer of the mouth. The operation to remove the upper left jaw took place on a yacht on Long Island Sound on July 1. In a second secret operation on July 17, other parts of the growth were taken out, and the president was fitted with an artificial jaw made of rubber. Three weeks later, Cleveland was well enough to address Congress. No one noted any change in the president.

One of the surgeons was W. W. Keen of Philadelphia. In 1921, Keen was attacked in some circles for failing to diagnose Franklin Roosevelt's paralyzed condition as polio. Keen, a surgeon, had been the nearest medical person to Roosevelt's summer home at Campobello.

Winston Churchill met seven presidents or men who would become presidents. Which was the first president that he met?

A Procession of Presidents

William McKinley. At the White House, McKinley hosted the newly elected member of Parliament in December 1899. McKinley was taken by Churchill's energy and intelligence. The first man Churchill met who would become president was Governor Theodore Roosevelt in Albany, New York, in December 1900. Roosevelt, at that time, was vice president elect.

Churchill was impressed by TR, but the feeling was not reciprocated. Roosevelt's daughter Alice later said:

> They were too much the same. Father was like a former debutante meeting the prize of the new season of debutantes.

Churchill met Woodrow Wilson at Versailles. He was turned off by Wilson's intransigence. He also disliked Herbert Hoover when they crossed paths in World War I.

Churchill was very close to FDR—his World War II ally whom he came to love. His relations with Truman were more formal, but he praised Truman as a president for his leadership during the cold war. Churchill developed a very close, almost avuncular relationship with Eisenhower—first in World War II and then when they were both heads of government. He met John F. Kennedy when Kennedy's father was ambassador to Great Britain. He would talk to JFK from his yacht in New York Harbor in 1961. He met Nixon when Nixon was vice president and was impressed by Nixon's grasp of world affairs.

Which president has been deemed by the American Conference Management Association to be "father of the conference or retreat center"?

Weekend Retreat

Dwight D. Eisenhower. As president of Columbia, Eisenhower believed there should be a retreat away from the university or business office to discuss problems. He persuaded Averell Harriman to allow use of his estate in Westchester County as a weekend retreat center. The practice caught on, and the American Conference Management Association now salutes Eisenhower's initiative.

Months before Churchill's Iron Curtain speech, this future president delivered an address that predicted the cold war—and gave a prescription for ending it. Who was this future president?

Returning Veteran

Richard Nixon. In January 1946, returning naval Lieutenant Commander Nixon told the audience at a Kiwanis club in Pomona, California, that Eastern Europe was increasingly under Soviet control, but if the West remained militarily strong and united, Communism would collapse in the face of a more productive free society. Nixon announced his bid for Congress a month later.

Winston Churchill suffered two life-threatening illnesses while visiting these two men. One was president at the time. The other would become president. Who were they?

"I'm at the End of My Tether"

President Franklin Delano Roosevelt and General Dwight D. Eisenhower. Just after Pearl Harbor, Prime Minister Churchill visited FDR at the White House. After Christmas day, Churchill suffered a small heart attack when trying to open a window in the Monroe bedroom. It was, however, announced only that Churchill had canceled meetings because of a cold. Three days later he took a train to Ottawa to address the Canadian House of Commons.

In December 1943, after ten exhausting days at the Teheran Conference with Stalin and Roosevelt, Churchill arrived at General Eisenhower's house in Algiers. "I'm at the end of my tether, Ike. You'll have to put up with me for a few days." Churchill incurred pneumonia that night, followed up by a slight stroke. He almost died. He rested at Eisenhower's Maison Blanche in Algiers and read some of Ike's Zane Grey Westerns. By Christmas he was well enough to sit up and enjoy a turkey dinner with Eisenhower.

Nine words from the most memorized speech in history were taken from a biography of another president that the author read in his youth. Who were the two presidents?

"That These Dead Shall Not Have Died in Vain"

Abraham Lincoln and George Washington. Lincoln took these words from Reverend Mason Weems's *Life of General Washington*. Lincoln had borrowed the book from a nearby farmer and had read it nightly for months. One night, after a torrential rainstorm, Lincoln discovered that water had seeped between the logs of his home and destroyed the book (Lincoln had to clear an acre field of logs to pay for the book). One page, however, in this ruined book was still legible. It was the last page showing a woodcut of General Washington kneeling before a monument marked "Valley Forge." Underneath were nine words: "That these dead shall not have died in vain." The words were permanently etched in twelve-year-old Lincoln's mind. Forty years later, he would say these very words at Gettysburg.

According to many historians, who was really the first president of the United States of America?

John the First?

John Hanson. The Maryland delegate to the Continental Congress was elected president in 1781, just before the time of Lord Cornwallis's surrender at Yorktown, Virginia. His official title was "President of the United States Assembled." While president, Hanson called for a national day of thanksgiving. President Washington, in 1787, would do the same.

Which president presented Elvis Presley with a government badge?

Agent Elvis?

Richard Nixon. In 1972, Nixon gave the pop idol a narcotics officer's badge and enlisted him in the war against drugs.

Which president staged a garage sale for White House furniture?

History for Sale

Chester Alan Arthur. Arthur professed dissatisfaction with the old furniture in the executive mansion. Sheraton chairs, Chippendale tables, and antique lamps were set out on the lawn and sold. Arthur was a devotee of Louis Tiffany, the interior designer, much of whose work was chosen for new appointments in the White House. More than eight thousand dollars was cleared from the mass sale of furniture in 1882.

Which president became bankrupt and penniless?

Down and Out

Ulysses S. Grant. In 1881, Grant moved from Galena, Illinois, to New York. He invested all his money in a brokerage firm, Grant and Ward. Because of disastrous speculation, the firm went bankrupt. A destitute Grant turned down an offer of $100,000 by P. T. Barnum to put his medals, trophies, and Civil War mementos on traveling exhibition. On the advice of Mark Twain, Grant turned to writing. His autobiography would earn a fortune after his death.

Since Eisenhower's heart attack in 1955, only two presidents have refused to make their complete medical reports available to the public. Who were they?

No News Is Good News?

John F. Kennedy and Bill Clinton. The failure to release their records spawned rumors. It is known that Kennedy suffered from Addison's disease. He had a kidney deficiency and needed constant medicine. Clinton dismissed the White House physician, who had recommended a medical examination. Political opponents circulated tales that both presidents had been afflicted with venereal infections.

Who is the only president to have his likeness on both sides of a coin?

Penny Portraits

Abraham Lincoln. Lincoln is depicted on both sides of the penny, although it requires a magnifying glass to see the visage of Lincoln sitting on his chair in the Lincoln Memorial. More than a billion pennies have been struck since 1951 with this design by Frank Gasparro, who also designed the Eisenhower dollar and Kennedy half-dollar. Gasparro's initials are on the right foot of the Lincoln Memorial.

Which president, as a youth, ran away to sea?

Starstruck?

James Garfield. From an early age, Garfield dreamt of being a sailor. At age sixteen, against his mother's objections, he went down to the Cleveland lakeside docks and tried to enlist on one of the ships. Turned down, he signed on with a canal boat, the *Evening Star*, that shuttled from Cleveland to Pittsburgh.

Which two presidents changed their first names when they were young men?

Name Change

Grover Cleveland and Dwight D. Eisenhower. Stephen Grover Cleveland was named after the Rev. Stephen Grover, who had preceded his father as minister in his Caldwell Presbyterian Church in New Jersey. By age nineteen, he began signing his name S. Grover Cleveland, and two years later he dropped the initial.

Eisenhower was named after his father, David Dwight Eisenhower. He was called by his middle name to avoid confusion. By the time he was at West Point, he had changed his name to Dwight David Eisenhower.

Which president had a stamp collection that sold for more than $200,000 after his death?

Philatelist President

Franklin Delano Roosevelt. As a youth in Hyde Park, Roosevelt was fascinated with faraway places. The fantasies were stirred by his mother. The Delano side of the family were merchant shippers who sailed all across the Pacific to ports in Asia. His collection increased through his Harvard days and then through his time as assistant secretary of the navy. As president, he received stamps from kings and heads of state—prize, first-release stamps. On his death in 1945, the collection, America's largest, was sold.

Which president gave away thousands of toothbrushes as gifts?

Ivory Polishers

Lyndon Johnson. LBJ had his best thoughts while performing the morning ablutions of shaving and brushing his teeth. So he figured that others might have their morning musings colored by memories of him if he gave visitors toothbrushes as mementos of their visits to the Oval Office or the LBJ ranch. Accordingly, he gave out LBJ toothbrushes with the presidential seal.

Which president had a heart attack in the White House but concealed his illness from the public?

Indisposed?

Chester Alan Arthur. In his last year at the White House, Arthur suffered a heart attack. Engagements were canceled. Meetings were halted. It was known that the president was indisposed, but the public never knew how serious his ailment was.

Interestingly, Eisenhower did have a heart attack in the summer of 1955, and he suffered a mild stroke in the fall of 1957. Both illnesses, however, were fully reported.

Which president once suggested cow dung as the weapons for a duel?

Bullshit?

Abraham Lincoln. In 1838, Whig State Representative Lincoln experienced a bitter campaign with James Shields, the Democrat. His losing opponent felt that Lincoln, with his attacks on Shields's integrity, had besmirched his character. He challenged Lincoln to a duel. The one challenged has the right to choose the weapons. Lincoln, half in jest, said: "Cow dung at twenty paces." The duel was eventually called off. Lincoln was never particularly proud of this incident.

Who is the only president to win a libel suit?

Six-Penny Prize!

Theodore Roosevelt. The former president was weary of recurrent rumors and allegations of his drunkenness. So he sued to put a stop to them. He brought suit in Marquette, Michigan, for the minimum amount of damages for statutory filing—six cents.

The defendant was George A. Newett, and the newspaper was the *Ishpeming Iron Ore*. Numerous dignitaries came to the Upper Peninsula to testify to TR's habits of moderation in alcohol. Among them were Admiral George Dewey, hero of the Spanish-American War; James Garfield, former cabinet secretary and son of the president; General Leonard Wood; Jacob Riis, the urban reformer; and former Secretary of State Robert Bacon.

Who was the only president to be made an honorary citizen of another country?

Pardon My French

James Madison. Congressman Madison accepted an honorary citizenship by the French Revolutionary government in 1796. Madison opposed President Washington's Proclamation of Neutrality in the war between France and Britain. Washington did not approve of Madison's acceptance of the honorific.

Which president had two species of fish and one land mammal named for him?

Odd Fish

Theodore Roosevelt. A new species of trout running in the rivers of northern California was named for him in 1910. The next year a tropical fish in Hawaii was given his name.

TR also took pride in *Cervus roosevelti*, a new species of elk in Wyoming.

Roosevelt, despite his duties of state, remained a naturalist all his life. In the Amazon jungle in 1909, he discovered new species of insects, birds, and one rodent.

Who was president when electricity was installed at the White House?

Shock-Proof?

Rutherford B. Hayes. Fixtures were installed, but Mrs. Hayes did not like them. She was afraid of receiving a shock when she touched the switches.

EDUCATION

Four presidents were academically elected to Phi Beta Kappa at their respective colleges. Who were they?

Whiz Kids

John Quincy Adams at Harvard in 1787 (the society that was established at William and Mary in 1776 began its Harvard chapter in 1781), Chester Alan Arthur at Union College in New York in 1848, Theodore Roosevelt at Harvard in 1880, and George H. W. Bush at Yale in 1948. (Herbert Hoover had the grades at Stanford, but the Phi Beta Kappa society did not honor those in engineering.)

Which president was assassinated en route to his college reunion?

Alumnus and Assassination

James Garfield was shot on July 2, 1881, at the Baltimore and Potomac Railway depot in Washington, D.C., by Charles Guiteau, a disappointed office seeker. Garfield was on his way to Williams College in Massachusetts for his twenty-fifth reunion. He wrote this ditty about Mark Hopkins, the president there when he attended:

> Mark Hopkins sat on a log
> he one side and the student t' other.

Tho' he was a theologue
he taught us like a brother.

Garfield survived another eighty days before dying of blood poisoning on September 19 in Elberson, New Jersey.

Which president founded a university?

"Mr. Jefferson's University"

Thomas Jefferson founded the University of Virginia in Charlottesville in 1819 and was its first rector. In the epitaph he wrote for his grave, Jefferson did not mention his presidency.

> Here lies buried Thomas Jefferson, author of the Declaration of Independence, of the Statute of Virginia for Religious Freedom, and Father of the University of Virginia.

Who was the only president to have been a professor at a women's college?

Petticoat Prof

Woodrow Wilson taught government at Bryn Mawr College outside Philadelphia, Pennsylvania. Although his pupils adored him, his wife encouraged him to leave and study for his Ph.D. at Johns Hopkins.

Who is the only president to have earned a postgraduate degree from Harvard?

"B" School Bush

George W. Bush earned his M.B.A. from Harvard in 1975. He studied harder than he had at Yale and did quite well. In the twentieth century, only six presidents had postgraduate degrees.

Who is the only president to earn a Ph.D.?

Doctor of Government

Woodrow Wilson went to Princeton to study to be a clergyman but didn't like it. He studied law instead. He didn't like the practice of law either and went to earn his doctorate in government at Johns Hopkins, where he earned his Ph.D. in political science in 1886. His thesis was *Congressional Government*. It was 333 pages long, and it was published by Houghton Mifflin. Interestingly, Wilson's foe Senator Henry Cabot Lodge was also a doctor of government, which he'd received at Harvard. The two men hated each other. Lodge helped defeat Wilson's League of Nations.

Which president turned down an honorary degree from Oxford University?

Nolo Contendere?

Former president Millard Fillmore, in 1853, was the chancellor of the University of Buffalo. He turned down an offer of an honorary doctorate of law by the Earl of Derby, chancellor of Oxford University. Fillmore wrote: "I have not the advantage of a classical education, and no man should, in my judgment, accept a degree he cannot read."

Who was the only president in the twentieth century not to attend college?

"Harricum"

Although Harry Truman studied business law briefly at Kansas City Law School in the 1920s, he never attended college or received a degree. He was, however, a great reader of American history. His favorite president was Polk.

In 1956, Oxford University gave him an honorary doctorate and addressed the man from Missouri as "Harricum Truman."

Which president received the most honorary doctorates?

"Honorary" Hoover

Herbert Hoover received more than fifty honorary degrees from American universities and more than twenty-five from foreign universities, not to mention the "freedom of the city" of more than a dozen municipalities, as well as hundreds of other medals, honors, and awards.

Which presidents attended military academies?

West Point 2, Annapolis 1

Ulysses S. Grant and Dwight D. Eisenhower both graduated from West Point. Grant was in the class of 1843 and Eisenhower in the class of 1915. The 1915 class was called "the year the stars fell" because so many in World War II would rise to be general officer rank. Both men had records studded with demerits for deportment and graduated in the middle rank of their class.

Jimmy Carter, class of 1947 at Annapolis (he graduated in an accelerated wartime class in 1946), placed in the upper tenth of his class. His confessed ambition was to become head of naval operations.

Which presidents, while alive, had colleges named after them?

What's in a Name?

Both General George Washington and General Dwight D. Eisenhower had colleges named after them. Washington had several. Washington College in Chestertown, Maryland, was founded in 1787; Washington had given it one hundred pounds. Washington and Lee in Lexington, Virginia, developed out of Washington Academy, which took the president's name after a gift from Washington in 1798. Washington and Jefferson in Washington, Pennsylvania, also emanated from a Washington Academy. It did not become a college until 1806.

Eisenhower University was established in Seneca, New York, in 1968. It closed its doors in 1986.

Jefferson Medical School should also be mentioned. This prestigious medical school in Philadelphia, Pennsylvania, opened as Jefferson Medical College in 1825, a year before Jefferson's death.

Which presidents attended universities outside the United States?

No Sheepskins

Bill Clinton, like his hero John F. Kennedy, whom he once met, attended university in England but did not earn a degree. John F. Kennedy went to the London School of Economics in 1935. Bill Clinton won a Rhodes Scholarship from Arkansas to Oxford in 1968 and 1969. Very active in student demonstrations against the Vietnam War, Clinton did not earn a degree.

Which president dropped out of Princeton, graduated from Harvard, and was awarded an honorary degree from Yale?

Ivy League Trio

John F. Kennedy entered Princeton in the fall of 1935 but dropped out at Christmas. He entered Harvard the next fall and received his degree in 1943. In 1962, as president, he received an honorary degree from Yale.

Which four presidents had law school degrees?

Presidential Pettifoggers

William Howard Taft graduated from the University of Cincinnati Law School in 1880, Richard Nixon from Duke Law School in 1936, Gerald R. Ford from Yale Law School in 1941, and Bill Clinton from Yale Law School in 1973.

Nixon graduated number three in his class. Ford placed in the upper third (a class that included Secretary of State Cyrus Vance, Sargent Shriver, and Supreme Court Justice Potter Stewart). Franklin Delano Roosevelt attended Columbia Law School but did not graduate.

Although he didn't graduate from a law school, Woodrow Wilson did study law as an undergraduate at Princeton after switching from theology. He practiced law briefly in Atlanta, and after he'd left the White House, he set up a firm with his former secretary of state called Wilson and Colby.

The Delta Kappa Epsilon fraternity lists five presidents as members. Who are they?

Deke Freaks?

One of the oldest college fraternities, Delta Kappa Epsilon proudly mentions Theodore Roosevelt, Rutherford B. Hayes, Gerald Ford, and both Bushes as its members. George W. Bush was president of the fraternity at Yale.

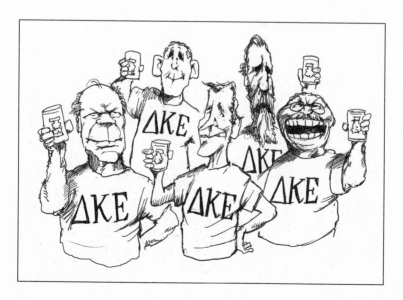

Which presidents were presidents of a college before entering the White House?

Ivy League Presidents

Woodrow Wilson was president at Princeton. He introduced the preceptorial method but failed to abolish the social eating clubs at Princeton during an eight-year term that ended when he ran for governor of New Jersey in 1910.

Dwight D. Eisenhower was president at Columbia from 1948 to 1950. He forbade the introduction of loyalty oaths. He later said his greatest accomplishments were persuading Nobel Prize–winning scientist Isidor Rabi to stay at Columbia instead of going to Princeton and football coach Lou Little to stay rather than going to Yale.

ELECTIONS

Which two presidents ran five times for the number one and two offices of the nation (president and vice president) and won four of those times?

FDR and RN

Franklin Delano Roosevelt, as the Democratic candidate for vice president in 1920, lost. The former assistant secretary of the navy and state senator was paired with Governor James Cox of Ohio. It was hoped that the Roosevelt name (Theodore Roosevelt had died in 1919) would add glamour to the ticket.

Roosevelt would then win four elections to the presidency.

Richard Nixon twice won as vice president with Dwight D. Eisenhower. Nixon was selected to balance Eisenhower in age (thirty-nine) and geography (California). Eisenhower liked Nixon because he was an internationalist (supporter of Truman's NATO and the Marshall Plan) who could appeal to the Taft wing because of his exposure of state department adviser Alger Hiss as a Communist.

Nixon would lose the presidential election to Kennedy in 1960 but win the election and reelection in 1968 and 1972.

Besides FDR, which three presidents received a plurality more than two times?

Tricky for Dick

Andrew Jackson had the plurality of votes in 1824, but the House of Representatives elected John Quincy Adams. Jackson would win election as president in 1828 and reelection in 1832.

Grover Cleveland won the presidential election in 1884 and again in 1892. In 1888, he lost reelection in the electoral college to Benjamin Harrison but won a plurality of the popular vote.

Interestingly, Richard Nixon also qualified. He lost the electoral college to John F. Kennedy in 1960, and most believe that he also lost the popular vote plurality narrowly. However, in the southern states of Alabama, Georgia, and Mississippi, Kennedy was not on the ballot. The states' Democratic Party, with Senators Harry Byrd and Richard Russell as the standard-bearers, beat the Republican Party's electors for Nixon. At the electoral college, the Democratic electors voted for Kennedy. The Democratic votes in those states were added to the Kennedy totals.

Nixon would win the presidency in 1968 and reelection in 1972.

In the nomination of this president, his supporters printed fake convention passes to pack the hall. Who was the president?

Winning Tickets?

Abraham Lincoln. The 1860 Republican convention was meeting in Lincoln's home state of Illinois; but those running the Chicago convention were friendly to Senator William Seward of New York, the leading candidate and most widely known Republican in the country. Lincoln's strategy was to attack none of the other candidates—Salmon Chase of Ohio, Edward McLean of Missouri, as well as Seward—so as to position himself as everyone's second choice.

If Lincoln was generally successful in making no enemies in preconvention maneuvering, not much enthusiasm was kindled for Lincoln himself.

Lincoln had legions of supporters in Illinois, but the convention chairman had allotted the Lincoln home-state partisans relatively few gallery seats in the "Wigwam" convention hall. Lincoln's managers overcame that by printing up forged tickets. The Lincoln supporters, armed with the counterfeit tickets, shook the hall with cheers as the votes for Lincoln rose with each ballot and launched the bandwagon to victory.

Who was the only president to defeat two other presidents in the same election?

"The Big Three"

For the early part of the twentieth century, "the big three" referred to the Ivy League football teams of Harvard, Yale, and Princeton.

In 1912, Democratic Governor Woodrow Wilson of Princeton defeated Republican President William Howard Taft of Yale and Progressive Party candidate and former president Theodore Roosevelt of Harvard.

Who was the only president to be preceded and succeeded by the same man?

The Cleveland Sandwich

Grover Cleveland was the incumbent president defeated by Benjamin Harrison in 1888, but Cleveland returned to beat Harrison in 1892. Grover Cleveland was the bread on either side of the Benjamin beef.

Who is the only president never elected as either president or vice president?

"There's a Ford in Your Future"

Gerald Ford was chosen vice president by the House of Representatives after the resignation of Spiro Agnew in 1973. Nixon had proposed Ford, which was approved by Congress under the terms of the Twenty-fifth

Amendment. Ford then succeeded President Nixon when he resigned in August 1974.

Which president won his first election to the local legislature by buying drinks for the constituents just before they voted?

Drinks Are on the House

George Washington lost his first two elections to Virginia's House of Burgesses by not buying drinks. The third time in 1758, Squire Washington was more generous to his neighbors and won.

Three presidents faced in an election major party candidates who were also residents of their home states. Who were the three presidents?

Home-State Advantage?

President Franklin Delano Roosevelt beat Governor Thomas Dewey of New York in 1944. Senator Warren G. Harding of Ohio defeated Governor James Cox of the same state in 1920.

In 1860, Abraham Lincoln of Illinois defeated Stephen Douglas of that state. But it was a four-man race with Lincoln, Douglas, John Breckinridge, and John Bell.

The first time soldiers were given the right to vote away from home made the difference in electing this president. Who was the president?

The Military Vote

Abraham Lincoln. In 1864, Congress passed the law allowing members of the military away from home to vote. President Lincoln had strongly backed the legislation; he was very popular among the enlisted men. That and the farm vote won him the election. The military vote for Lincoln exceeded 70 percent.

The chairman of the Nixon "secret" fund that triggered controversy in the national election of 1952 was the son of a president. Who was the president?

Blind Trust?

Herbert Hoover. Herbert Hoover Jr. was the chairman of the Nixon fund. He organized the expense fund to pay for air travel to California and other expenses in a way that Nixon would not know the identity of the donors. In that sense, it was secret.

Governor Adlai Stevenson in 1952 also had a fund in Springfield, Illinois, to assist him with expenses; he used the fund to buy suits, among other things. Stevenson, however, did know the names of his contributors.

Which general was the winner when he faced four other generals in a presidential election?

General Election

General James Garfield, a Republican, in 1880 defeated fellow Union Army General Winfred Hancock, a Democrat. General James Weaver was the candidate of the Greenback Party; General Neil Dow was the candidate of the Prohibition Party; and General John Wolcott Phelps was the candidate of the American Party.

Which election was finally settled by the Supreme Court?

Vote Verdict

In perhaps the most acrimonious and contested election in history, the Supreme Court voted six to three to reaffirm the Florida secretary of state's awarding of the state to Governor George W. Bush against Vice President Al Gore in December 2000. The Supreme Court overturned a decision of the Florida Supreme Court that had asked for a revote.

This president—in case of defeat—intended to immediately appoint his opponent, if victorious, to the position of secretary of state. Then the president as well as the vice president would resign in order that the secretary of state could take office as president right away. Who was the president?

No Lame-Duck President?

President Woodrow Wilson in 1916. He intended to appoint his Republican opponent, Governor Charles Evans Hughes of New York, as secretary of state the day after his defeat. For a long time on election night, it seemed that Wilson might do just that. But California came in for Wilson; and when morning came, it was clear that Wilson had won. (Wilson, a doctor of government, believed that the long "lame-duck" period from November to March was debilitating and he respected Hughes. But one wonders whether Wilson would have done the same had his opponent been someone like Theodore Roosevelt or Senator Henry Cabot Lodge, both of whom he despised.)

Who was the only president to be elected unanimously thy the electoral college?

Father of Our Country

George Washington. Everyone in the Constitutional Convention knew that the position of presidency in that charter was written with General Washington in mind. Washington did not run for a third term because he wanted to ensure the democratic transition of office.

Who were the only two presidents elected by the House of Representatives?

The House and the White House

Thomas Jefferson and John Quincy Adams. In an election fluke, Jefferson and Aaron Burr, the Democratic Party's candidates for president and vice president, received the same number of electoral votes in 1800.

In the House of Representatives, Alexander Hamilton threw the Federalist vote to Jefferson. Burr never forgot. He would later kill Hamilton in a duel.

In 1824, John Quincy Adams ran second to General Andrew Jackson in the popular vote, but Jackson did not win the majority of electoral votes. Henry Clay, the Speaker of the House, swung his support to Adams and was later appointed secretary of state. Clay would, however, deny that any deal had been made.

FAMILY

Which president had fourteen children?

Prolific President

John Tyler had fourteen children who lived to maturity. By his first wife, Letitia Christian, he had three sons and four daughters before he became president. Letitia died in 1842.

The president later married his second wife, Julia Gardiner—who was thirty years younger than he was. Seven children were born to that union—five boys and two girls. The youngest, Pearl born in 1860, would live until 1947, more than a century after Tyler left the White House.

Incidentally, John Tyler was a great-great-great uncle of Harry Truman.

A president-elect's son was killed by the train that was to carry the family to his inauguration ceremonies in Washington. Who was the president?

Pierce's Pain

Franklin Pierce. Pierce's eleven-year-old son, Benjamin, was run over by a train near Andover, Massachusetts, on January 6, 1853, a few months before Pierce's inauguration. The boy had run across the tracks and was killed instantly by the locomotive. Mrs. Pierce interpreted it as an act of

God punishing her husband for running for president. Two other children had died in infancy. The result was Mrs. Pierce's estrangement from her husband and increasing dependence on alcohol by the president.

Who was the first divorced president?

Movie Star Marriage

Ronald Reagan. Reagan was the first divorced man to serve in the White House. The divorce between him and movie star Jane Wyman became final in 1948. They had separated in 1947. The underlying cause for the breakup was Reagan's increased involvement with the Screen Actors Guild.

Wyman was the Academy Award winner for her portrayal of the deaf-mute in *Johnny Belinda* in the 1940s, when Reagan was president of the Guild. Later Wyman would star as the matriarch in the CBS TV series "Falcon Crest." By this first marriage, Reagan had two children: Maureen (1941) and Michael (adopted in 1945). One girl baby died in 1947—the strain of which some think led to the separation. No mention of Jane Wyman is found in the Reagan Presidential Museum in California.

In 1952, Reagan married Nancy Davis. They had two children: Patti (1952) and Ronald Prescott (1958).

Which president's daughter would marry the Speaker of the House?

Prince Nick?

Alice Roosevelt, the eldest child of Theodore Roosevelt, married Congressman Nicholas Longworth of Ohio in 1906. "Princess Alice," as she was nicknamed in Washington, was the belle of Washington in the early years of the twentieth century. The headstrong beauty married the much older congressman, who was a dapper blade in Washington circles. Bald as a cue ball, Longworth nevertheless made a striking presence. The marriage, however, had its difficulties.

Longworth, who served as Speaker of the House during President Hoover's administration, had the reputation of a philanderer. He was once teased by a congressional colleague, who, while rubbing his hand over Longworth's bald head, said: "Your head feels just like my wife's behind." Longworth then felt his bald pate and replied: "By Jove, it does!"

Which president had the first grandchild born in the White House?

James Madison? . . .

Thomas Jefferson's daughter Martha bore the president a grandson in the White House in 1806. His name was James Madison Randolph after Jefferson's secretary of state and the future president.

The first granddaughter born in the White House was Letitia Tyler in 1842, daughter of Robert Tyler and granddaughter of John Tyler. Robert Tyler would later serve as treasurer of the Confederacy where his face adorns now-worthless Confederate bonds. Letitia was named after her grandmother, the first lady, who had recently died in the White House—the first first lady to do so.

Who was the first president to have his daughter marry in the White House?

Princess Alice

Theodore Roosevelt. His firstborn, Alice, married Congressman Nicholas Longworth in the White House on February 17, 1906. Alice was perhaps the only person who could outstage her father, even though she said of him: "Father always wanted to be the center of everything—the bride at a wedding—the corpse at a funeral." Alice was the only one of his children to inherit his quick mind and independent spirit. At the White House wedding, many of the lady guests wore accents of "Alice blue" in honor of Alice's favorite color. After a lavish wedding, the Longworths honeymooned in the newly independent Cuba.

Which president had a great-grandfather who fought at Gettysburg and is buried in the Gettysburg cemetery at which Lincoln spoke?

Private Nixon

Richard Nixon. George Nixon III fought as a Union private from Indiana and died in the Battle of Gettysburg. His grandson, Frank, was the father of the president.

Who was the only president to have a child born in the White House?

Dandy Delivery

Grover Cleveland. His second daughter, Esther, was born in the White House on September 9, 1893. Incidentally, the last of Cleveland's children, Francis Grover, born in 1903, is still alive at the writing of this book.

Which president once broke off his engagement?

Abe in a Blue Funk

Abraham Lincoln was engaged to Mary Todd. The wedding date was set for March in 1840, but Lincoln broke off the engagement. Lincoln, a manic-depressive, had suffered fits of melancholy throughout that year.

It is a tribute to the oft-maligned Mary Todd that even though she had been jilted she kept faith that the relationship would revive.

The short, buxom Mary Todd had no shortage of suitors in Springfield, Illinois. One caller was none other than Stephen Douglas, who would become Lincoln's famous political rival. At one soiree Mary Todd was asked by a woman friend why she gave the cold shoulder to rich gentlemen visitors, preferring the ungainly Lincoln.

"I'd rather marry a good man of mind and bright prospects for fame and power than all the gold stones of the world."

The brother of one president once roomed in a boardinghouse with a brother of another future president. Name the two presidents.

Fraternal Friends

Vivian Truman, the younger brother of Harry Truman, once shared a boardinghouse room with Arthur Eisenhower, the older brother of Dwight. The businessmen, both about twenty-two, were working at the time in Kansas City, Missouri.

"Mad Anthony" Wayne was one of George Washington's favorite generals and was an ancestor of which president?

A Mad Dash?

Through his mother Hannah Milhous, Richard Nixon was descended from Anthony Wayne. Interestingly, one of Nixon's daughters now lives in Wayne, Pennsylvania, outside of Philadelphia, which is named for the

Revolutionary War general. Near Wayne there is an inn named for him, as well as a hotel and a house where he once lived.

When General Washington was positioned by the Hudson River in 1779, he called in Wayne.

Said Wayne: "I'll storm Hell, General Washington, if you will plan the assault!"

And Washington replied: "Perhaps, my dear General Wayne, we had better try Stony Point first!"

Which president's grandson married a president's daughter?

Love at First Sight?

Dwight D. Eisenhower. On December 22, 1968, in New York, Julie Nixon, daughter of President-Elect Nixon, married David Eisenhower (Dwight David Eisenhower II), grandson of President Eisenhower. They had first met at General Eisenhower's inauguration in 1953, when each had been a little over four years old. David had been fascinated with a black eye that Julie had recently acquired.

When David was attending Amherst College, his grandmother, Mamie Eisenhower, suggested he look up Julie, who was attending Smith College nearby.

What two widowers were elected president?

Pining Presidents?

The first was Martin Van Buren. His wife, Hannah Hoes Van Alen, died in 1819, almost two decades before Van Buren entered the White House. Interestingly, Van Buren did have one serious romance as a widower. She was Ellen Randolph, granddaughter of Thomas Jefferson. Van Buren was then a senator twenty years Ellen's senior. The relationship was very serious—for a time.

The second was Chester Alan Arthur. He married Ellen "Nell" Herndon in 1859. She was the daughter of Captain William Herndon, who in

1857 went down with his ship, *The Central America*, after seeing to the safety of his passengers. She died in January 1880 of pneumonia and so was never to witness her husband's vice presidential nomination and election later that year.

Andrew Jackson's wife, Rachel, died after his election in 1828 but before his inauguration in 1829.

Which president experienced the tragedy of his mother and wife dying on the same day?

Twin Tragedies

Valentine's Day 1884 was a day of unbearable tragedy for Assemblyman Theodore Roosevelt. On that day, his mother, Martha Bullock Roosevelt, died of typhoid fever, and his wife, Alice Lee, died of Bright's disease. Two hearses drove to the Fifth Avenue Presbyterian Church for the service.

Devastated in his grief, Roosevelt went West to work as a cowboy, and his infant daughter, Alice Lee's namesake, went to live with Roosevelt's sister.

In 1886 Roosevelt would marry his childhood friend, Edith Kermit Carow.

Which two presidents experienced the death of a son who was living at the White House at the same time?

Mansion Mourning

Willie Lincoln, Abraham Lincoln's third son, died in the White House of typhoid fever in 1862. It followed by ten years the death of his second son, Edward. Willie was a bookish child and perhaps the closest to his father in affections. Willie's death at age twelve shattered his mother. At the time Lincoln was going to make the Gettysburg Address, she tearfully pleaded that if he went, Tad, the youngest son, who was suffering from a one hundred–degree fever, would die.

Calvin Coolidge Jr. died from a freak accident. The sixteen-year-old developed an infection playing tennis without socks. His death during the presidential campaign of 1924 devastated his parents. "The power and the glory of the presidency died with him," said Coolidge.

Which president had two siblings who served jail sentences?

Family Felons

Bill Clinton's half brother Roger served in prison for selling drugs. The president pardoned Roger as he left office in January 2001. Not so well known is half sister Diane Dwire Welch, who did time for a bank robbery in Virginia. Presidential candidate Clinton kept her secreted in a motel under an alias during the presidential campaign of 1992.

Which president had a marriage annulled?

Nullified Nuptials

The thirty-year-old freshman congressman John F. Kennedy married Palm Beach socialite Durie Malcolm in February 1947 at a justice of the peace's chambers. Joseph Kennedy, the congressman's father, was irate. The one-year-older Episcopalian divorcée was not acceptable. The marriage was quietly annulled, and the page announcing the marriage in the Palm Beach County registry was expunged. The event is listed in the Blauvelt family genealogy. The bride's mother's family were Blauvelts.

Which president's brother prevented the leg amputation of the future president?

Brotherly Love?

Dwight D. Eisenhower might have suffered the same fate as the character played by Ronald Reagan in *King's Row*—if not for his older brother Edgar. Dwight Eisenhower developed an infection in his right leg after a fall in his freshman year in high school in Abilene, Kansas. The doctor recommended amputation. Ike overheard the doctor's conversation with his parents.

Ike made his brother swear an oath to stop the amputation. "I'd rather die than lose my leg." The brother camped outside Ike's bedroom. The doctor said: "Son, you are going to murder your own brother." Edgar was resolute. Ike and his leg survived.

Which president never married because of his fiancée, who after an argument committed suicide?

The Bereaved Bachelor

James Buchanan. The only bachelor president never married. His fiancée, Anne Coleman, daughter of Lancaster, Pennsylvania, millionaire Robert Coleman, was beautiful and rich. They quarreled; she broke the engagement and went to Philadelphia to stay with cousins there. She died at age twenty-three in 1819 of an overdose of laudanum. The twenty-eight-year-old Buchanan said: "Life now presents to me a blank . . . my happiness buried with her in a grave." Some historians, however, have speculated that Buchanan was gay.

Which president's father was attorney general of the central states?

Noblesse Oblige

William Howard Taft. One of the most public-service-minded families in American history is the Taft family of Cincinnati, Ohio. President and Chief Justice William Howard Taft was the son of Alphonso Taft, who served as attorney general and secretary of war, a post that William Howard Taft would later hold.

President Taft's son, Senator Robert A. Taft, twice tried to become the Republican presidential nominee in 1948 and 1952; he was the Senate majority leader when he died in 1953. The president's grandson, Robert Taft, was also a senator; and his great-grandson, Robert Taft, is now governor of Ohio.

Which president's great-great-grand uncle was John Knox, the Scottish founder of Presbyterianism?

Presbyterian President?

James K. Polk was proud of his Scottish heritage. Through his mother, Jane Knox, he claimed the famous Calvinist preacher as his collateral ancestor. Born and raised a Presbyterian, he studied at a Presbyterian school in Tennessee and read the gospels in Greek.

He married Sarah Childress, a Methodist, and converted to her religion at his deathbed.

Which president is deemed by genealogists to be related to eleven other presidents—George Washington, John Adams, James Madison, John Quincy Adams, Martin Van Buren, William Henry Harrison, Zachary Taylor, Ulysses S. Grant, Benjamin Harrison, Theodore Roosevelt, and William Howard Taft?

Patrician President

Franklin Delano Roosevelt was not only a fifth cousin of Theodore Roosevelt and fourth cousin of Grant and Taylor; he was also a distant cousin to eight other presidents, not to mention a seventh cousin of Winston Churchill.

Which president had a second cousin who preceded him as president?

Cousin James

Not Franklin Delano Roosevelt, who was a fifth cousin of Theodore (although FDR married Teddy's niece).

It was Zachary Taylor, who shared a great-grandfather with James Madison. When his cousin was commander in chief in the War of 1812, Taylor defended Fort Harrison in a determined Indian assault.

By his cousin, President Madison, he was then brevetted a major. At age twenty-eight, he was the youngest major in the U.S. Army.

FIRST LADIES

Which first lady was a British subject and the daughter of a British army officer?

Tory Daughter

Elizabeth Kortright Monroe was a daughter of Captain Lawrence Kortright of the Royal British Army. He was a wealthy Tory merchant in New York City, who saw most of his fortune confiscated during the Revolution. Monroe, who was ten years older, married the elegant Elizabeth in 1786. Monroe was then a member of the Continental Congress from Virginia.

Which first lady rescued the Gilbert Stuart portrait of George Washington from a fire in the White House?

Dauntless Dolley

Dolley Madison. In the War of 1812, the Royal Marines landed in Washington and burned the White House. Before they did so on that August day, Dolley Madison arranged the safe transport by carriage of certain treasures, including the Washington portrait. She wrote her sister:

> I am still here within sound of cannon. Mr. Madison comes not. May God protect him! A wagon has been procured. I insist on

working until the large portrait of George Washington is secured.
It requires to be unscrewed from the wall.

Who served longest in the role of hostess or first lady at the White House?

Hostess with the Mostest

Dolley Madison. First she took over the arrangements for the widower
Thomas Jefferson. Jefferson, though he came from a patrician background, had built up his new Democratic-Republican Party by stressing
his egalitarianism. At the newly built president's house, he decreed no

protocol—no ranking of precedence at tables. It was catch-as-catch-can in seating. Secretary of State James Madison's wife soon set him straight that protocol was necessary to preserve a sense of order and dignity of the office. When Madison followed Jefferson's two terms with eight years of his own, she served as first lady in her own right.

But her leading hostess days were not over. When her husband died, she took her niece Elizabeth to meet crowned heads of Europe and then maneuvered Elizabeth into marrying the widower Martin Van Buren's son John. Elizabeth took over the first lady duties in the Van Buren White House, but it was Dolley who had the final say on invitations.

Which first lady was the first president of the National Society of the Daughters of the American Revolution?

Dowager Dame

Caroline Scott Harrison, the wife of Benjamin Harrison, was first lady when the DAR was established in 1890. The society's members are composed of those who can prove they have an ancestor who had military service in the War of Independence. It was incorporated a year later, and the first lady was elected to be the first president general. Her husband was the grandson of President William Henry Harrison. Mrs. Harrison also erected the first Christmas tree at the White House.

Which first lady was the aunt of her husband's second wife?

Bridal Boycott

Caroline Scott Harrison came down with tuberculosis in 1892. Her niece, Mary Scott Dimmick, a widow, filled in as first lady. After Benjamin Harrison left the White House, he married Mary Scott Dimmick in 1896. Harrison's grown children, resentful at the ex-president's marriage to someone twenty-five years younger than he was, did not attend the wedding.

Who was the only first lady committed to a mental institution?

Mad Mary?

Mary Todd Lincoln was committed to an asylum by her only surviving son, Robert, in 1875. The death of her son Willie was the first breaking point. The assassination of her husband unhinged her further. When her son Tad died in 1871, she began hallucinating about seeing him. She was put into an institution in Batavia, Illinois. Two years later she was released to the care of her sister, Mrs. Edwards, in Springfield, Illinois.

Which first lady was responsible for bringing the cherry blossoms to Washington?

Flower Girl

Helen Herron Taft in 1912 arranged for the planting of three thousand Japanese cherry trees in the Washington Tidal Basin. With the Japanese ambassador, Mrs. Taft personally planted the first two saplings on March 27, 1912.

Which first lady was investigated by Congress for traitorous conduct?

Mary Todd a Traitor?

Mary Todd Lincoln was, perhaps, the most unpopular first lady. Congress was suspicious of her loyalties to the Union in the Civil War. Four of her brothers fought for the Confederacy, and three of them had died.

On top of that, she ran up huge expenses in purchasing china and furniture for the White House.

The president was compelled to appear in the Senate and say: "It is untrue that any of my family holds treasonable relations with the enemy." There is no evidence for any pro-Confederacy sympathy by Mrs. Lincoln. She was staunchly pro-Union.

Which first lady refused to allow her husband to be alone with another woman?

Mary and the Green-Eyed Monster

Mary Todd Lincoln never let her husband be alone with another woman. When Mrs. Lincoln learned that her husband, in his visit to inspect the Army of the Potomac, had been alone with Mrs. Grant, she threw a fit. The president had gone to the tent headquarters of Grant, and when Grant wasn't there, he had talked amiably with Grant's wife.

Later, when Mrs. Lincoln saw Mrs. Grant, she flew into a tantrum. Because of that, Mrs. Grant turned down an invitation to Ford's Theater on April 14 and perhaps saved her husband's life.

Which first lady won a seat in the House of Representatives?

The Gentle Lady from Virginia?

In 1844, Dolley Madison was seen sitting in the gallery. Congressman Saunders from North Carolina introduced a resolution to grant Mrs. Madison a seat within the House chamber. It was passed unanimously.

Which first ladies were divorcées when they married their husbands?

Gay Divorcées?

Florence "Flossie" King DeWolfe, a divorcée with one son, married Warren Harding, five years her junior, in 1891. Her shrill nagging of her husband was said to have impelled him to seek the company of other women.

Elizabeth Ann Bloomer divorced her first husband, William Warren, in 1947; she married Gerald Ford a year later at Grace Episcopal Church in Grand Rapids, Michigan. Their marriage was as happy as the Hardings' was unhappy.

Which first lady interviewed her future husband for a newspaper before he became president?

"Inquiring People Want to Know"

Jacqueline Bouvier was hired as the inquiring camera girl for the *Washington Times Herald* shortly after graduating from George Washington University in 1951. That year she interviewed Congressman John F. Kennedy. A romance followed, and they were married in 1953 in Newport, Rhode Island.

Who was the first first lady to write her memoirs?

Pen Lady

Eleanor Roosevelt's first autobiographical work, *This Is My Story*, was finished in 1937. Later she wrote *On My Own* (1958), which was syndicated in the *Ladies' Home Journal*, and the *Autobiography of Eleanor Roosevelt* (1961). A prolific writer, for years she had a daily syndicated column, "My Day."

Which first lady was a teacher who was pursued by her former pupil until she agreed to marry him?

Powers and Her Pupil

Abigail Powers Fillmore. Millard Fillmore was a student in 1819 at Baptist Academy near Moravia, New York. At nineteen, he was Abigail Powers's oldest student. He had a crush on his teacher from the very beginning, and he married her after a seven-year courtship in 1826.

Which first lady had more than five hundred pairs of gloves?

"The Ransacker of Fifth Avenue"

That was the term used to describe Mary Todd Lincoln after a shopping raid in New York.

A compulsive shopper, Mrs. Lincoln had a particular fondness for shoes and gloves. In one four-month period in 1864, she purchased three hundred pairs of gloves.

Which first lady moved thirty-five times in thirty-five years?

A House Is Not a Home

Mamie Doud Eisenhower was an army wife. So she got used to frequently "decamping" and "pitching up in a new tent." Her travels with General Eisenhower took them to San Antonio, Texas; Camp Colt in Gettysburg; Fort Leavenworth, Kansas; and Fort Meade in Maryland; not to mention Panama and the Philippines.

In 1948, General and Mrs. Eisenhower—then living in New York, where he was president of Columbia University—bought a parcel of land in Gettysburg. The courthouse clerk asked Eisenhower why he wanted to buy the land in Gettysburg when they already had a house in New York. General Eisenhower explained they wanted to build a permanent home.

Said Ike: "In the army, we never had a real home, and one day we want to take a piece of earth and return it to God better than we found it."

Which first lady caught her widower husband by running backward into his arms and fainting?

Welcoming Widower

Julia Gardiner Tyler, in 1844, as daughter of State Senator David Gardiner, was a guest of the president on the USS *Princeton*, the first screw propeller ship. On this February outing, the highlight was to be the firing of the new naval gun called "the Peacemaker." It exploded, and Secretary of Navy Abel Upshur and David Gardiner were killed. At the blast, a hysterical Julia backpedaled and collapsed in the president's embrace. Julia, a vivacious, striking brunette from one of New York State's oldest families, had been long interested in the widower president. She had earlier shocked New York society by posing as "the Rose of Long Island" for a department store ad. A lover of the stage, she often acted in skits. She married the president in June 1844.

Who is the only first lady to have earned a law degree?

"Portia Faces Life"

Hillary Rodham Clinton, after graduating from Wellesley, went to Yale Law School, where she met her husband. She later taught at the University of Arkansas Law School and then became a partner of the Rose Law Firm in Little Rock. Her mentor there was Webster Hubbell. Hubbell, who was appointed by President Clinton to a high position in the Justice Department, later went to jail for irregularities in his billings as a lawyer.

Which first lady used the East Room of the White House to hang out wet clothes to dry?

Hung Out to Dry

The first first lady to live in the White House was Abigail Adams. It was called the President's House, and the Adams family moved in in March 1800. Because of the spring rains, she used the East Room to dry wet clothes.

Which first lady was called "the presidentress"?

The Other Twenty-Eighth President

Edith Bolling Wilson. Woodrow Wilson suffered a stroke in Pueblo, Colorado, in September 1919 while campaigning for the League of Nations. Edith made decisions on behalf of her paralyzed husband in the last year and a half of his presidency. As he slowly regained his tenuous hold on his responsibilities, his wife maintained what she called "Mrs. Wilson's stewardship." She did so on advice of a doctor, who said that the blood clot in his brain would dissolve if he was spared the task of decision making—but that resignation would cause his death.

In 1920, rumors were so rife about his incapacity that a delegation came from the Senate to see the president, who sat in a dark room with a blanket over his paralyzed side and leg.

Senator Albert Fall, a Republican foe of the president, upon leaving said: "We're praying for you, Mr. President."

"Which way?" was Wilson's dry reply.

Which first lady was once national president of the Girl Scouts?

Lou the Leader

One of the most learned of our first ladies was Lou Hoover. A graduate of Stanford, Hoover was a scholar in Latin and proficient in French as well as Mandarin Chinese. She served as president of the Girl Scouts while her husband was secretary of commerce under Harding and Coolidge.

Who was the first first lady to possess a college degree?

Learned Lucy

Lucy Webb Hayes graduated from Wesleyan Female College in Cincinnati, Ohio. A devout Methodist, she would pray every morning with her husband and ended each day by singing hymns.

Which first lady liked to smoke a corncob pipe?

Pipe-Smoking Peggy

Margaret "Peggy" Smith was the wife of Zachary Taylor. She prayed that her career soldier of a husband would not win the presidency. A semi-invalid first lady, she stayed on the second floor smoking her pipe and letting her daughter assume the duties of White House hostess.

Another wife of a general also liked the pleasures of a corncob pipe—Rachel Jackson. She died just before Jackson entered the White House.

Which first lady had built in the White House a raised platform upon which she could sit to receive guests at a reception?

Queen Julia

Julia Gardiner Tyler, in her weekly levee, would greet Washington women on this raised platform that suggested the aura of a throne. Naturally, it drew criticism, particularly from those women who were much older than the first lady, who was only in her twenties. They also sensed regal airs in Mrs. Tyler's special carriage drawn by four white horses, which she used for driving around Washington.

Which first lady would stage "the silent treatment" to any member of the White House staff who displeased her?

Bess the Boss

Bess Truman. Harry Truman called his wife "the boss." She ran a very tight ship at the White House. After years of the laissez-faire stewardship of Eleanor Roosevelt, the staff had to get used to Mrs. Truman, who would occasionally rub a white glove across door tops. Staff members who did not do their job received "the silent treatment."

Which first lady studied at a university abroad?

La Belle Jacqueline

Jacqueline Bouvier Kennedy spent a year at the Sorbonne in Paris after two years at Vassar. She then graduated with an arts degree at George Washington University. When she went to France on a state visit in 1963 with the president, the French-speaking first lady captivated Paris. President Kennedy said to the cheering Parisians: "I am the husband of Jacqueline Kennedy."

Which first lady once assisted in the defense of two Black Panthers accused of murder?

Saint Hillary

Hillary Rodham Clinton. Yale Law School student Hillary Rodham worked on the development of a defense that brought acquittal of the Black Panthers. One of the acquitted defendants later tortured and murdered a fellow Black Panther.

Which first lady always wore a turban hat with foot-high feathers?

Divine Dolley

Dolley Madison reigned as the dowager queen of Washington society long after she left the White House in 1817. The widowed Dolley returned in 1836 to star on the Washington scene until her death in 1849. She wore, long after they went out of fashion, dresses in the "empress" style, and her trademark was the turban hat with feathers.

In the twentieth century, which first lady most hated her time in the White House?

No Home at the White House

According to Margaret Truman Daniels, it was her mother, Bess Wallace Truman. Bess hated Washington and yearned to return to the Wallace home in Independence, Missouri. She didn't mind being the wife of a senator, because then she spent most of her time in Missouri. However, she found the fishbowl life of the White House unbearable. She was angered by Truman's decision to run for a full term in 1948; some estrangement resulted from this decision.

Which first lady inaugurated the Easter Egg Roll on the White House lawn?

Bunny Hop

Lou Hoover inaugurated the Easter Egg Roll in 1930. The first children to attend were those of the White House staff.

Two first ladies were married in foreign countries. Who were they?

Americans Abroad

The first was John Quincy Adams's wife, Louisa Johnson. At age twenty-two, she wed Adams in London in 1797. They were married at All Hallows Barking parish in London. She was the daughter of an American consul, Joshua Johnson, then serving in London. Adams was a diplomat, who had been appointed by Washington and was then serving his father, President Adams.

The second one was Edith Carow, Theodore Roosevelt's second wife. She also was wed in London in 1886. Edith was a childhood friend of Theodore Roosevelt. They were wed at St. George's Church of Hanover Square in London.

Which first lady wore a low-neck, lacy décolletage gown—making the daring style the most fashionable in the country?

Jazzy Julia

Julia Dent Grant shocked Washington with the gown's display of her bosom. Critics said it was to take attention away from her cross-eyes. Nevertheless, the style swept the nation.

As first lady, Mrs. Grant was a lavish entertainer at the White House. One of her dinners ran to twenty-nine courses. She was, in addition, a staunch advocate of women's rights and befriended feminist Susan B. Anthony.

Who was the first first lady to receive honorary degrees before she entered the White House?

Doctor Hoover

Lou Hoover was given many honorary degrees before her husband's election to the presidency. In addition, she was decorated by the king of Belgium for her relief work. She could read several languages and authored some books.

Which first lady lived the longest?

Long Live the Queen

Mrs. Truman died at age ninety-seven in Independence, Missouri, of congestive heart failure on October 18, 1982. Harry had died ten years before, on December 26, 1972.

Which first lady was nicknamed "Sahara Sarah"?

The White House and the "Wet House"

Sarah Childress Polk was a strict Methodist who banned alcohol and card playing from the White House. Dolley Madison used to ease the thirst of visitors to the White House by offering them drinks at her nearby Octagon House, both before and after their visits to the White House. For its wine and whiskey hospitality, Dolley's house was nicknamed the "Wet House."

Which first lady was the first person, besides Alexander Graham Bell and his assistant, to use a telephone?

No Busy Signal

Lucy Webb Hayes. Bell came to the White House to test his invention. Mrs. Hayes then talked over the phone to Bell's assistant, Watson.

Which first lady frequently suffered epileptic seizures at White House state dinners?

Epileptic Ida

Ida McKinley. Contrary to protocol, President William McKinley would sit beside his wife at state dinners. When his wife had a fit, he would place a napkin over her head and let the dinner proceed as if nothing had happened. McKinley's attentive conduct toward his semi-invalid wife was considered saintly by American women.

Which first lady delivered a speech in sign language to the Gallaudet School for the Deaf in Washington?

"Silent" Grace

Grace Coolidge. In her opening commencement address to the graduates, Mrs. Coolidge said:

> My husband, who is known as "Silent Cal," has forbidden me to speak as first lady. I have obeyed that restriction. I am not "speaking" today, am I?

Which first lady said about her husband: "I have a presentiment that he will meet with a sudden and violent death."

Mary's Nightmare

Mary Todd Lincoln. Once her husband told her of a dream shortly before his election to the presidency that after a day of politicking he saw in the mirror a double image of himself—the second image was pale like a dead man's. His wife's interpretation of it was that he would have two terms as president but die in his second term.

Lincoln, a couple of days before he was shot, also dreamt that he heard moaning and crying. He went downstairs and saw a bier on the mantle in the East Room. Someone told him it was the body of the president.

On the day of his assassination, Lincoln and his wife took a ride. Lincoln reached out to hold his wife's hand and said: "Dear, I have never felt so happy in my life."

Mrs. Lincoln responded: "You said the same thing just before our boy Willie died."

Which first lady made a point of washing her own undies?

Panty Penance

Pat Nixon. According to her daughter, Julie, Mrs. Nixon said:

> There are so many in the White House ready to wait on you hand and foot. I do this to remind myself who I am and where I came from.

FOOD AND WINE

Which president had a 1,235-pound cheese presented to him at the White House?

Big Cheese

Thomas Jefferson. On New Year's Day 1802, President Jefferson was greeted with this gift with the sign: "The greatest cheese in America for the greatest man in America." Israel Cole of Cheshire, a town in the Berkshire Mountains in western Massachusetts, had transported the cheese to Washington in a cart pulled by six horses.

Which nineteenth-century president ran up a $25,000 wine tab?

Enologist

Thomas Jefferson. Jefferson spent about $25,000 a year in the purchase of French and Italian wines.

A connoisseur of fine wines, Jefferson preferred the lighter Bordeaux to the heavier burgundy or Italian wines. He also encouraged Italian grape growers to emigrate to America. In his library, there were books on grapes and wine.

In 1981, a case of wine marked for Thomas Jefferson was found in a Rothschild cellar. In the French Revolution, the cache of red Bordeaux wine was hidden from authorities and put behind a newly erected wall. It was sold for six figures.

A popular candy bar is named after a daughter of a president. Who was the president?

La Bambina?

Grover Cleveland. Baby Ruth, the chocolate candy bar, is named after his daughter Ruth, not after the Yankee immortal. She was born in Washington, D.C., in 1891, four years before George Herman Ruth's birth in Baltimore, Maryland. When Cleveland was inaugurated the second time and moved back into the White House, the blonde tyke became a favorite of the press corps. Ruth Cleveland died in 1904 from diphtheria.

Which president generally rejected meat and preferred fish?

Other Fish to Fry

George Washington. The old general did not refuse to eat meat out of some principle or scruple. Rather, it was that he couldn't chew beef very well with his ill-fitting dentures. He did not miss meat in his daily fare because he preferred fish—particularly trout and especially the salt codfish that swam in the Chesapeake Bay and the Potomac waters near his Mount Vernon estate.

Which president had a bourbon named for him?

"Taught to the Tune of a Hickory Stick"

Andrew Jackson. "Old Hickory" is the name of a popular bourbon and the nickname of our seventh president. Hickory is the sturdiest of native American woods and was the popular choice for canes. Tough and gnarled hickory sticks were used to administer beatings of recalcitrant youths in the woodshed. The lean and gaunt frame of Jackson, together

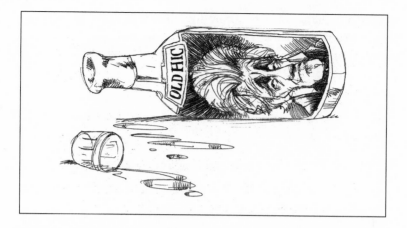

with his "take no prisoners" approach, made the sobriquet fit. Because Jackson was regarded as a "man's man," the distillery company gave their bottle of sour mash Jackson's nickname.

Which first lady first served ice cream at the White House?

Dolley's Dessert

Dolley Madison. Who else? She is often given credit for inventing ice cream, but she did not. The Italians did, but she popularized it in America by serving it in the White House first when she was the official hostess when the widower Jefferson was president. It was a favorite of Jefferson. Later in Madison's White House, it was a featured dessert delicacy.

Which president was responsible for bringing the first pasta-making machine to this country?

Pasta President

Thomas Jefferson. Imperia, Italy, is the site of the Agnesi Historical Museum of Spaghetti (it is also the home of Italy's oldest pasta manufacturer). There resides an order by Thomas Jefferson for a pasta-manufacturing machine. Jefferson used the machine, but he could not get his Virginian neighbors to eat the product. So the machine rusted away in his barn.

Which first lady once had menus for a White House dinner printed on satin?

Imperial Elegance

Mrs. Ulysses Grant. Julia Dent Grant had menus printed on satin for a dinner honoring a Russian prince.

Which president cherished his own prize recipe for vegetable soup?

Soup's On!

Dwight D. Eisenhower. Food was just fuel for the career soldier. For a husky man, he was a light, almost disinterested, eater. He did, however, enjoy grilling steaks for friends visiting him at Camp David. He also took pains in preparing for them his own recipe for vegetable soup, which he would stew the day before serving. He would hand out his recipe for the soup as a souvenir.

Which president is credited for inventing the "Gibson" martini?

Martini Maestro

Herbert Hoover. The dour Republican president is the improbable popularizer of garnishing gin martinis with onions instead of olives. His preference for onions began in World War I when Hoover was pressing the Germans to allow him behind the lines to administer food to the war-ravaged and starving civilians. Hoover and U.S. Ambassador Hugh Gibson met the Germans for lunch in the German embassy in Brussels. Many martinis were consumed during the discussion of arrangements. The meeting would be continued at the U.S. embassy that evening. Because more martinis would be served and the Americans wanted to keep their heads clear, Gibson proposed the Americans would drink faux martinis of ice water that would be garnished with onions to differentiate them from the real "olive" martinis. The ploy was successful, and Hoover was granted passage behind the lines.

Later in the White House, President Hoover would mix up a batch of gin martinis and serve them with onions, calling them his "Gibsons," named after his friend Hugh Gibson.

Which president is credited for helping to initiate the "coffee break" tradition?

Crullers and Coffee

The midmorning coffee break began to emerge mostly in Northern cities following the Civil War. The custom had spread through Union camps. Some social historians have credited a young William McKinley with starting this tradition. McKinley had attended Allegheny College at the age of fourteen and taught school at age sixteen. He passed himself off to be twenty when he enlisted, though he was only eighteen. While waiting for his commission, he got the idea of taking around coffee in a cart to the soldiers who had been up since before six o'clock. Because of that, McKinley was made commissary sergeant at age nineteen. The ten o'clock coffee that the Ohio regiments had initiated under McKinley spread to Pennsylvania and then the Massachusetts regiments. That was the genesis of the coffee break.

Which first lady's teetotaling habits earned her the nickname of a nonalcoholic beverage?

"Lemonade Lucy"

Lucy Webb Hayes. Both President Rutherford Hayes and his wife were firm teetotalers. At state dinners, lemonade or other nonalcoholic drinks were served. Detractors dubbed her "Lemonade Lucy," but the Woman's Christian Temperance Union hailed her. She did make one exception: wine was served at a reception honoring a Russian grand duke in 1877.

Which president invented the dumbwaiter?

Wine Shipper?

Thomas Jefferson was intrigued by labor-saving devices. He developed a dumbwaiter to haul goods from his cellar to the dining room in Monticello. A shaft connected the basement to the dining room, and he rigged the conveyor cart with ropes and pulleys. The dumbwaiter often sent bottles as well as root vegetables stored in the cellar up to the dining room.

Which president smoked twenty cigars a day?

The Stogey Soldier

Ulysses S. Grant. The general was first a pipe smoker but switched to cigars in the Civil War. When a journalist described him as one with a cigar always clenched in his mouth, people from all over the North began sending him cigars. He gave some to enlisted men he encountered on the front lines, but mostly he smoked about twenty or more a day himself. The smoking, no doubt, contributed to the mouth cancer that would end his life.

Which president always had fish for breakfast at the White House?

Sailor's Fare

Franklin Delano Roosevelt. FDR liked cod, mackerel, and herring for breakfast. The yachtsman and former assistant secretary of the navy said fish was "sailor's fare."

Which president's words became the signature slogan of a famous brand of coffee?

"Good to the Last Drop"

Theodore Roosevelt. While president, Roosevelt stopped at the Maxwell House in Nashville, Tennessee. As he finished his after-dinner coffee, he wiped his mouth and uttered: "Good to the last drop." The family sold their brand to General Foods.

A candy manufacturer dedicated a new flavor to a president of the United States. Who was the president?

Blueberry Bean

Ronald Reagan. Jelly Belly, the manufacturer of jelly beans, created a blueberry jelly bean in time for Easter in 1986. The new bean was dedicated to President Reagan, who would give out jelly beans in his office. Blueberry was the president's favorite fruit flavor. He liked anything with blueberries in it—pancakes, muffins, or just a bowl of blueberries.

GEOGRAPHY

Which president was given a castle in Scotland?

General Delivery?

Dwight D. Eisenhower. For his services to freedom in World War II, General Eisenhower was delivered the deed to Culzean Castle in Scotland. On his death, it was given back to Scotland and taken over as a hotel administered by the Scottish National Trust. Eight rooms and a dining room, called the Eisenhower Suite, are a featured part of the castle. General Eisenhower gave many mementos and relics of his war years to the castle, and they are on display. The castle stands on a cliff overlooking the Atlantic Ocean in Ayrshire, some thirty miles south of Glasgow.

Which president had a capital of a foreign country named for him?

"Free at Last, Free at Last"

James Monroe. In 1817, the American Colonization Society purchased Upper Guinea in West Africa for the purpose of resettling freed blacks in the United States. On August 15, 1824, the name of the country was changed to Liberia (meaning freedom), and the capital city was named Monrovia, in honor of President James Monroe.

For which president is the highest mountain in North America named?

Mount McKinley

In 1913, Hudson Strick scaled the 20,300-foot mountain in Alaska and named it for the assassinated president, William McKinley. It was dedicated as a national park in 1917. The park is full of glaciers and is host to bear, caribou, and mountain sheep.

Who was the first sitting president to visit a foreign country?

Panama Pilgrimage

Theodore Roosevelt. President Roosevelt visited the nation of Panama in 1906. He arrived on the USS *Louisiana*, which left New York City. At Roosevelt's instigation, the Panama province revolted and declared independence against the country of Colombia. The fledgling republic then negotiated a treaty with the United States for the building of the canal. Colombia, for years, had exasperated the United States with its up-and-down demands that, at times, came close to extortion. The purpose of Roosevelt's visit was to inspect the progress of the canal construction.

Who was the first president born outside the thirteen original states?

Log Cabin Location

Abraham Lincoln. Lincoln was born in a log cabin near Hodgenville in Hardin County, now Larue County, Kentucky, to Nancy Hanks Lincoln. The twenty-five-year-old Nancy died nine years later. Though she could not read or write, she was remembered by her son as intelligent. "All I am or hope to be, I owe to my sainted mother." Lincoln was estranged from his father, Tom Lincoln, and did not attend his funeral in 1851.

Who was the first president to visit Alaska?

Pleasure Cruise?

Warren G. Harding. President Harding was the first president to visit Alaska, as well as Canada, while president. He and Mrs. Harding sailed on the USS *Henderson*, a navy ship, and visited Metlakatla, Alaska, and two weeks later Vancouver, British Columbia. On the return trip to San Francisco, Harding took ill on July 27. He died on August 2 in the Palace Hotel. The doctors concluded that the president had suffered a stroke. In 1930, a convicted swindler, Gaston Mean, published a sensational book, *The Strange Death of President Harding*. It suggested that Harding had been poisoned by his wife. His theory has been dismissed by historians.

Who was the first sitting president to visit Europe?

Peace Pilgrimage

Woodrow Wilson. President Wilson was the first president to cross the Atlantic Ocean. He sailed on the SS *George Washington* on December 4,

1918, and arrived in France on December 13. Wilson attended the Versailles Conference to work out peace negotiations, following the end of World War I.

Which president has a river in a foreign country named for him?

Roosevelt Rio

Theodore Roosevelt. Roosevelt Rio, the river in Brazil, was originally called the River of Doubt. In 1913 and 1914, Roosevelt went to Brazil and made a fifteen-hundred-mile expedition collecting plant and animal specimens. He almost died of malaria. Brazil renamed the River of Doubt in his honor.

Which president's name and signature are on the moon?

Men on the Moon?

Richard Nixon. On the L.E.M. vehicle left behind on the moon by the *Apollo 11* astronauts is a plaque that states:

> Here men from the planet Earth first set foot upon the moon in July 1969 A.D. We came in peace for all mankind.

Above the names and signatures of astronauts Edwin Aldrin, Neil Armstrong, and Michael Collins is the name and signature of Richard Nixon.

Who was the only president to address the Houses of Parliament in London?

"Marxism Is on the Ash Heap of History"

Ronald Reagan. His close political ally and friend, Prime Minister Margaret Thatcher, arranged the appearance. In 1982, President Reagan delivered a historic speech imploring the free world to seize the initiative and end the cold war. The defensiveness of détente would be replaced by a ringing affirmation of freedom—free market, free speech, free assembly. He issued the prediction "Marxism is on the ash heap of history."

Who was the first president to be born west of the Mississippi?

West Branch

Herbert Hoover. The thirty-first president was born in West Branch, Iowa, in 1874. The town is now the site of the Hoover Memorial. Both the president and his wife are buried there.

Which president picked the precise Potomac area that is now Washington, D.C., as the capital for the new nation?

Surveyor Washington

George Washington. In 1790, the long dispute between the North and South on the location of the new capital was settled. Alexander Hamilton and Thomas Jefferson made their deal. In return for Jefferson and his followers' support for a Federal Bank and assumption of debt, Hamilton would agree to a capital somewhere along the border of Maryland and Virginia. Until that agreement, the leading candidate was a town on the Susquehanna River west of York, Pennsylvania, which is now named Columbia. Once a Potomac River site was established, Washington picked the area adjacent to what was then called Georgetown, Maryland.

Which four presidents have state capitals named after them?

"Sing Praises to His Name"

Thomas Jefferson, James Madison, Andrew Jackson, and Abraham Lincoln.

Jefferson City, Missouri, was incorporated in 1825; Madison, Wisconsin, in 1846; Jackson, Mississippi, in 1833; and Lincoln, Nebraska, in 1869.

Interestingly, the state capital in Lincoln houses the only unicameral (one legislative chamber) legislature in the nation.

A fashionable section in Washington, D.C., is named for which president who once lived there?

Cleveland Park

Although the city of Cleveland, Ohio, is not named for Grover Cleveland, Cleveland Park in Washington, D.C., is. This section in northwest Washington is between Wisconsin and Connecticut Avenues, north of the Calvert Street Bridge. When President Cleveland was defeated in 1888, he moved temporarily to the slightly higher area. It was not densely settled, and people started calling it "Cleveland Park."

Which president has one state, seven mountains, eight streams, ten lakes, thirty-three counties, and one hundred twenty-one towns and villages named for him?

Father of Our Country

George Washington, of course! The first town named for George Washington was Forks, North Carolina, which changed its name to Washington in 1775. Washington, Georgia, was the first town incorporated with the name of Washington.

Interestingly, the only monument erected to Washington while he was alive stands in Baltimore, Maryland.

Who is the only president born in New York City?

Native New Yorker

Theodore Roosevelt. On October 27, 1858, the future president was born in a brownstone, four-story house at 28 East Twentieth Street in New York City.

Which four presidents traveled together to a foreign country?

Cairo Congregation

President Ronald Reagan and former Presidents Richard Nixon, Gerald Ford, and Jimmy Carter flew in Air Force One to attend Anwar Sadat's funeral in Cairo in October 1981.

Which two presidents were born on the same street?

Street Site

John Adams and John Quincy Adams were both born on Franklin Street in Braintree (now Quincy), Massachusetts.

Inaugurations

Which president gave the longest inaugural address—an hour and fifty-five minutes?

Lethally Long-Winded?

William Henry Harrison, on March 4, 1841, rode up to the Capitol on a white horse. The sixty-eight-year-old general—then hatless and coatless

93

despite freezing weather—delivered his lengthy address. That night the first Whig president celebrated at three inaugural balls. He caught a chill and died a month later of pneumonia. In January, he had delivered a prophetic foreword in his home state of Ohio:

> Perhaps this may be the last time I have the pleasure of speaking to you on earth. I will bid you farewell.

Who was the first president to be inaugurated in the U.S. Capitol in Washington?

Half-Finished Capitol—Half Divided Country

Thomas Jefferson took the oath in the Senate chamber. Only the north wing of the Capitol building had been completed. His predecessor, John Adams, refused to attend.

State militias had gathered in Maryland and Virginia in fear of conflict as the House of Representatives met to elect the new president. It would be Jefferson—the only incumbent vice president to defeat an incumbent president. The Federalists, after twelve years, had been swept out of the highest office.

Jefferson tried to allay fears and seek unity by opening his inaugural address with:

> We are all Federalists. We are all Republicans.

Which president had to borrow money to pay for his travel to his inauguration?

No Wherewithal for Washington

George Washington had to borrow six hundred pounds from Richard Conway of Virginia to pay for his trip to New York City in 1789. The "land-poor" general complained of a season of low-yielding crops in his letter to Conway.

Who gave the shortest inaugural address?

A Spent President

A weary and ailing President Franklin Delano Roosevelt delivered a five-minute address from the balcony of the White House on January 20, 1945, to one of the smallest crowds in recent times. He would die on April 12.

Who is the only president not to use the word I in his inaugural address?

First Person?

Theodore Roosevelt, for whom self-effacement was not a virtue, surprisingly is the only president not to use the first person pronoun in his inaugural address of 1905.

Which president wore Abraham Lincoln's ring during his inauguration ceremony?

Ring Bearer

Theodore Roosevelt. Roosevelt's secretary of state, John Hay, had been Abraham Lincoln's private secretary. Hay, who was given possession of the ring by Mrs. Lincoln, presented it to Roosevelt for use in his swearing in in 1905.

Which three presidents took office with the most former presidents still alive?

Five Alive

When Abraham Lincoln took his oath in 1861, former Presidents Martin Van Buren, John Tyler, Millard Fillmore, Franklin Pierce, and James Buchanan were alive.

President Bill Clinton also had that distinction in 1993. Richard Nixon, Gerald Ford, Jimmy Carter, Ronald Reagan, and George H. W. Bush were still living.

Clinton's successor, George W. Bush, also had five living former presidents. Nixon had died in 1994, but Clinton was then an ex-president.

Which two presidents refused to participate in the inauguration ceremonies of their successors?

Adams Adamant

The two Adamses—father and son—boycotted the inauguration ceremonies of their successors—Thomas Jefferson and Andrew Jackson.

John Adams later reconciled with his old friend since their days in the Continental Congress. John Quincy Adams did not reconcile with Jackson, never saying a good word about the old general.

Which two presidents were sworn in by a previous president?

"Do You Solemnly Swear? . . ."

The first was Calvin Coolidge; in 1925, Chief Justice William Howard Taft swore him in. Then in 1929, Taft delivered the oath to Herbert Hoover. Taft had been appointed chief justice by Warren Harding. Coolidge's speech in 1925 was heard by twenty-five radio stations and an audience of twenty-three million people.

Which future president was drunk and collapsed when he gave his inaugural address as vice president?

Alcoholic Andy?

The new vice president, Andrew Johnson, while taking his oath in the Senate chamber, was clearly drunk. His face was flushed and his stance wobbly. He harangued about his lowly beginnings. Johnson was not, nev-

ertheless, known to be a heavy drinker (two of his sons, however, were alcoholics). The Tennessee governor was recovering from a bout of typhoid fever and had doctored himself with brandy.

Which president traveled incognito to Washington at night for his inauguration ceremonies?

Stealth of the Night

Abraham Lincoln. When Lincoln was en route to Washington for his inauguration, both the U.S. Secret Service and private detectives discovered what they believed was a plot to assassinate him as he passed through Baltimore.

It had been announced that Lincoln would speak in Harrisburg, Pennsylvania, on February 22, spend the night there, and then leave the next morning for Baltimore and Washington.

He made his speech in Harrisburg according to schedule, but instead of spending the night there, he slipped out the back door of the hotel that evening at six o'clock, and, disguised in an old threadbare overcoat and a soft wool hat such as he had never worn before, Lincoln was driven to an unlit railway coach. A few minutes later, an engine was whirling him away to Philadelphia, and the telegraph wires in Harrisburg were cut immediately so that the information would not be relayed to the would-be assassins.

At Philadelphia, the Lincoln party had to wait for an hour to change trains and stations. In order to prevent recognition during that time, Lincoln and Allan Pinkerton, the famous detective, drove through the streets of the city in a darkened cab.

At 10:55 P.M., leaning on Pinkerton's arm and stooping so as not to draw attention to his height, Lincoln entered the station by a side door. He carried his head bent forward and had his old traveling shawl drawn close so that it almost covered his face. In that guise, he crossed the waiting room and made his way to the rear section of the last sleeping car on the train, which one of Pinkerton's aides, a woman, had cut off from the rest of the car by a heavy curtain and reserved for her "invalid brother."

In the early hours of February 23, the train carrying the president-elect arrived in Washington, and Lincoln was met and taken unobserved to the Willard Hotel.

Which first lady wore an old dress to her husband's inaugural ball?

Secondhand Rosalyn

Rosalyn Carter. In recent history, the first ladies have all had a new gown for the occasion. Many of the dresses are in the Smithsonian.

Mrs. Carter, in keeping with her husband's decision to walk up Pennsylvania Avenue, wore an old gown she had used for a ceremony as wife of the governor of Georgia. President Carter, who formally changed his name from James to Jimmy, tried to introduce a less formal note to the presidency. He wore cardigans in TV appearances from the Oval Office and at first disdained the use of Air Force One.

One president's most frequently quoted line in his inaugural address is said to have been drawn heavily from a previous president's speech. Who are the two presidents?

"Ask Not . . ."

"Ask not what your country can do for you; ask what you can do for your country" is perhaps the most frequently quoted line from an inaugural address. John F. Kennedy's words resemble what Warren G. Harding said in 1916: "In the great fulfillment we must have a citizenship less concerned about what the government can do for it and more anxious about what it can do for the nation."

Ted Sorensen, who drafted Kennedy's inaugural address, said he was not aware of the Harding speech.

Who was the only president inaugurated in New York?

Wall Street Washington

George Washington. The first president took his oath on April 30, 1789, on the balcony of the Senate chamber at Federal Hall on Wall and Nassau Streets. Washington had arrived by boat up the Hudson River. The oath was delivered by Chancellor Robert Livingston of New York.

Chief Justice John Marshall swore in his cousin as president, a relative whom he didn't like and rarely spoke to. Who was the man?

Un-Civil Ceremony

Thomas Jefferson was a Randolph on his mother's side. So was John Marshall. They were second cousins. Marshall was a Federalist and a bitter opponent of "Jeffersonian democracy." In fact, there had been some maneuvering by some Federalists to make Chief Justice Marshall president in the murky situation following the bitter 1800 election that had to be decided by the House of Representatives.

Last Words

Name the president who said these last words: "I've always loved my wife. I've always loved my children. I've always loved my country."

A Soldier's Farewell

Dwight D. Eisenhower. The dying general at Walter Reed Hospital called his son, John Eisenhower, on the phone. John was staying in a suite on a floor below him.

When John came to the room, he found his father prone in an oxygen tent. "Pull me up, Johnny," he said.

Then General Eisenhower delivered the words with his wife also present; he then slipped into a coma and died a short time later. The date was March 28, 1969.

Name the president whose last words were these: "The only limit to the realization of tomorrow is our doubts of today."

Not Doubts but Dreams

Franklin Delano Roosevelt. Actually these were not his last spoken words. Those were: "I have a terrific headache." The words of hope were found on his legal yellow-lined tablet. It was the last line he had written for a speech to a Jefferson/Jackson Day dinner, in which he would mostly talk

100

about the plans for the new United Nations. He had gone to Warm Springs, Georgia, for a rest. Roosevelt had been drafting the address while having his portrait painted. He died on April 12, 1945.

Name the president who said these last words: "I love you for all eternity."

Love Conquers All

James K. Polk. His last words were addressed to his wife, Sarah, on June 15, 1849, at his home, Polk Place in Nashville, Tennessee. The fifty-three-year-old former president had been enjoying a triumphal tour of the South since he had left the White House in March. Sarah Childress Polk had been his best friend and chief adviser in his presidency. They had no children.

Name the president who said these last words: "Please put out the light."

Lights Out

Theodore Roosevelt. On January 5, 1919, at his home at Sagamore Hill in Oyster Bay, New York, Roosevelt went to bed at 11:00 P.M. after telling his valet, James Amos, "Please put out the light." He died in his sleep of a coronary embolism five hours later. That day he had written an article for the *Kansas City Star* that attacked President Wilson's proposal for a League of Nations.

Name the president who said these last words: "This is the last of earth. I am content."

Died in Harness

John Quincy Adams. On February 21, 1848, Congressman Adams spoke these words at the U.S. Capitol building. Minutes before he had cast a very loud no vote against a bill to honor generals in the Mexican War, which he opposed. He then suffered a stroke, and the former president was carried into the Speaker's room, when he spoke his last words. He slipped into a coma and died two days later, February 23, 1848. He was eighty years of age.

Name the president who said these last words: "I have tried so hard to do right."

Principled President

Grover Cleveland. These were the last words of one of the most principled presidents ever to occupy the White House. They were spoken at his home in Princeton to his wife on June 24, 1908. Cleveland had accepted responsibility for an illegitimate child because the other suspected fathers were married. Cleveland had vetoed the Civil War pension bills, when he had not served in the Civil War. Incidentally, a future president was living nearby, Woodrow Wilson, president of Princeton University. Their relations were not cordial. A lecturer in public affairs, Cleveland had clashed with Wilson on university policy. Cleveland was seventy-one.

Name the president who said these last words: "It is God's way. His will, not ours, be done."

"Thy Will Be Done"

William McKinley. He said these words on September 13, 1901, the day before his death in a hospital in Buffalo, where he had been taken after he had been shot on September 6. The cause of death was gangrene caused by the bullets shot by the assassin Leon Czolgosz, an anarchist. He would be buried at his home in Canton, Ohio. Czolgosz was executed in the electric chair at Auburn State Prison in New York on October 29, 1901. Czolgosz's last words were: "I killed the president because he was the enemy of the people—the good working people—I am not sorry for my crime."

Name the president who said these last words: "Sir, I wish you to understand the true principles of government. I wish them carried out. I ask nothing more."

Death in the White House

William Henry Harrison. The sixty-eight-year-old general realized he was losing his fight against pneumonia. He said these words to the doctor and those around him on April 4, 1841, shortly after noon. Episcopal services were read in the East Room of the Executive Mansion, where his body was laid in rest.

Media Milestones

Who was the first president to have a telephone on his desk in the White House?

Desk Phone

Herbert Hoover. He had the phone installed three weeks after he moved into the White House. Previously there had been a phone in a booth adjoining the president's office.

Who was the first president to broadcast a speech on radio?

Banner Day

Warren G. Harding. President Harding, at the dedication of the Francis Scott Key Memorial at Fort McHenry, Baltimore, delivered an address on "The Star-Spangled Banner" transmitted by a Baltimore radio station on Flag Day, June 14, 1922.

Harding was also the first president to have a radio. It was installed in a bookcase in his study on the second floor.

Which president was the first to be telecast in color?

Class Reunion

Dwight D. Eisenhower. The old general addressed his fortieth reunion of the class of 1915 at West Point on June 6, 1955. The address was carried the next day on NBC's program, the "Home Show."

Which president was the first to be filmed?

Candidate Cal

President Calvin Coolidge was filmed on the White House grounds in September 1924. The famous radio and film pioneer Lee De Forest did a newsreel that day of the three candidates in the 1924 presidential election. John W. Davis, the Democratic candidate, and Robert La Follette of the Progressive Party were the others.

Who was the first president to conduct a press conference?

"Mr. President . . ."

Woodrow Wilson. A week and a half after he was inaugurated, Woodrow Wilson, on March 15, 1913, held a press conference. Before that, press interviews had been limited to selected and favorite newsmen.

Who was the first president to deliver a speech on television?

"Fair" Reception

Franklin Delano Roosevelt delivered remarks to open the New York World's Fair on April 30, 1929, from the Federal Building on the Egyptian Grounds. The event was televised by the National Broadcasting Company.

Who was the first president to have a televised press conference?

Ike Live

Dwight D. Eisenhower. On January 19, 1955, President Eisenhower held a news conference that was covered by both newsreels and television. He answered questions about Red China, Formosa, and trade with Communists. It was covered by Fox Movietone on NBC.

Who was the only president to place a telephone call to the moon?

Long-Distance Charges?

Richard Nixon, on July 19, 1969, placed a call to the lunar expedition module that was on the surface of the moon. He congratulated the three astronauts of *Apollo 11* on their moon landing and had a conversation with astronaut Neil Armstrong.

MEMORABLE SAYINGS

Which president said: "A man who has never gone to school may steal from a freight car, but if he has a university education, he may steal the whole railroad"?

Trustbuster

Theodore Roosevelt. Roosevelt was the first president to take on big business. In the days when big monopolies, called "trusts," in railroads, steel, and oil were emerging, Roosevelt combated them. He was not antibusiness and did not side with journalists like Ida Tarbell and Lincoln Steffens on the left, whom he called "muckrakers." Roosevelt said that both big business and big labor should be bridled for their excesses.

Which president said: "I have only two regrets: I didn't shoot Henry Clay, and I didn't hang John Calhoun"?

Antagonistic Andy

Andrew Jackson. The cantankerous Jackson never was one to repress his views. He had killed one man in a duel, and he wished, similarly, that he had shot Clay, the leader of the Whig Party and his most formidable opponent in Congress.

John Calhoun resigned as vice president under Jackson to run for the Senate. Calhoun opposed the executive imperiousness of "King Andrew." At the White House, Jackson, looking at the states righter, Calhoun, said as a toast: "To the Union." Calhoun replied: "To the Union. Next to liberty most dear."

Which president said, "I only know two tunes: 'Yankee Doodle Dandy,' and I don't know the name of the other"?

Tin Ear

Ulysses S. Grant. General Grant was no lover of culture, despite the efforts of his wife, Julia, to make him go to the theater and attend recitals. This was Grant's dry comment on music.

Which president, when he was called two-faced in a debate, said in reply: "Now if I had two faces, would I be wearing this one?"

Two-Faced?

Abraham Lincoln. Senator Stephen Douglas accused Lincoln of being two-faced in his policy toward the extension of slavery in the territories. Lincoln, in his reply in the debate, opened his remarks with this light rejoinder, which brought chuckles from the crowd.

Which president said: "I have no trouble with my enemies. I can take care of my enemies. But my damn friends—my goddamn friends. They're the ones that keep me walking the floor at night"?

God Save Me from My Friends

Warren G. Harding. As the Teapot Dome scandal about oil leases steamed up, Harding said this about his profiteering friends. Harding was personally honest but was exploited by his business cronies.

Which president said: "The Republicans have fun, but they don't want people to see it. The Democrats, even when they are not having fun, like to appear to be having fun"?

"Eat, Drink, and Be Merry"

Richard Nixon. The insightful remark came from a very private person who was not demonstrative in public. He directed the remark at himself, as well as Republicans in general.

Which president coined the adage: "You can't change horses in the middle of the stream"?

The Farm Vote

Abraham Lincoln. President Lincoln was considered a goner for his reelection campaign in 1864. Thaddeus Stevens, the congressman from Gettysburg, declined a VIP invitation to attend the battlefield ceremonies in November 1863, saying: "Let the dead [Lincoln] bury the dead."

Experience was Lincoln's key advantage for reelection. He composed the homey maxim: "You can't change horses in the middle of the stream" to reinforce that asset. The analogy went over very well with the farm vote, which Lincoln carried. That and the soldiers' vote helped him win the election.

Which president said of himself: "Some folks are silly enough to have formed a plan to make a president of the U.S. out of this clerk and clodhopper"?

"Clodhopper?"

William Henry Harrison. He said this when he was a clerk of the common pleas in Cincinnati in 1838. His mention of this relatively low post omitted his impressive credentials as heroic general, congressman, state senator, territorial governor of Indiana, and U.S. minister to Columbia. He would be elected president two years later.

Which president wrote: "The art of making love muffled up in furs in the open air with the thermometer at zero is a Yankee invention"?

Brumal Bundling

John Quincy Adams. The dour Yankee president revealed his droll side. This diplomat and poet had a comic touch too.

Which president, when asked to submit a synopsis of his life, wrote: "My life is contained in one line of Thomas Gray's Elegy in a Country Churchyard: *the short and simple annals of the poor"?*

"Blessed Are the Poor . . ."

Abraham Lincoln. The artistic answer reveals the shrewd mind of a politician who knew that the retelling by people of his reply would be a vote getter.

Which president said that he wanted the following as his epitaph: "Whenever he found a thistle, he plucked it and planted a flower in its place"?

"With Malice Toward None, with Charity for All"

Abraham Lincoln. "Magnanimous" described the president, who said those poetic words in his second inaugural address: "With malice toward none, with charity for all."

During the Civil War, President Lincoln was besieged with appeals for soldiers caught in the machinery of military discipline. Such appeals were usually supported by letters from influential people. One day Lincoln found on his desk an appeal from a Union Army private without any supporting documents.

"What? Has this man no friends?" exclaimed the president.

"No sir," said the adjutant. "Not one."

Lincoln sighed, "Then I will be his friend."

Calhoun had once suggested that General Jackson should have been hanged for his brutality toward Indians in Florida. Jackson wanted to turn the tables on Calhoun.

Which president said: "The idea that I should become president seems to me to be too visionary to require a serious answer"?

The Very Idea! ...

Zachary Taylor. This was the general's answer to the Whigs who wanted the popular general to run against Martin Van Buren. He would later accept the Whig Party (National Republican Party) presidential nomination in 1848 and win.

Which president, who had been a Civil War general, said: "Fighting wars is like courting girls: those who make the most pretensions and are the boldest win"?

Marital Arts

Rutherford B. Hayes. As a young man in Ohio, the handsome Hayes, who didn't drink or smoke, was not without vices. He had an appetite for the ladies.

Which president made this comment about politicians: "Three things can ruin a man—money, power, and women. I have never had any money. I never wanted power, and the only woman in my life is up at the house right now"?

Pursuit of Office, Not Women

Harry Truman said this in 1961. Of course, he had wanted power and had sought a political career. The rest is true. Truman was an honest man, even though the corrupt Prendergast machine of Kansas City had been the instrument of his political success.

Which future president said to General Eisenhower: "There comes a time, General, when you have to shit or get off the pot"?

Dick's Demand

Richard Nixon. Vice presidential candidate Richard Nixon said this in a phone call to Eisenhower in September 1952, a couple of days after Nixon had delivered what came to be known as the "Checkers" Speech, which defended the so-called "secret fund."

In his televised address, filmed live in Seattle, Nixon set out all his financial records—certified by an accountant. The speech brought out the information that Adlai Stevenson, the Democratic presidential candidate, also had a fund for expenses, where he knew the identity of the donors, unlike Nixon, and that John Sparkman, the Democratic vice presidential candidate, had his wife on his senate payroll.

The telegrams that flooded the Republican National Committee were almost unanimous in support. Yet General Eisenhower was silent. Nixon's earthy statement was the result. Eisenhower flew to West Virginia, where Nixon was speaking. Ike embraced the tearful Nixon saying, "He's my boy."

Which president said: "Four-fifths of all our troubles in this life would disappear if we would only sit down and keep still"?

Silent Cal

Calvin Coolidge. The Yankee president was legendary for his reticence. Reporters questioned after he left church: "What was the sermon about, Mr. President?" "Sin," was the answer. "What did he say about it?" asked reporters. "He was against it," was Coolidge's laconic reply.

A woman in a receiving line at the White House once said to Coolidge: "Mr. President, I bet my husband I could make you say more than two words to me." "You lose," was Coolidge's reply.

Which president said of another president: "He means well but means well feebly"?

"Feeble" Minded?

Theodore Roosevelt said this of William Howard Taft. Roosevelt, who picked Taft in 1908 as his successor, would run against him in 1912.

Which president said: "I gave my enemies the sword for my own destruction"?

"Die by the Sword . . ."

Richard Nixon. Nixon believed that Watergate gave his enemies on the left the weapons to destroy his administration. The opposition to the Vietnam War—even though the Nixon Doctrine proposed and initiated the gradual withdrawal of U.S. troops from Southeast Asia—aroused passions that hadn't been seen in this country since the Civil War.

MILITARY
AFFAIRS

Which president served as a general on active duty after he left the White House?

"Old Soldiers Never Die"

Only one president, after he left office, was called back into active military service. That was George Washington. In 1798, as friction with former Revolutionary War ally France intensified, President John Adams appointed Washington as lieutenant general, head of all United States armies. The appointment of Washington, who was a world-respected figure, was a psychological as well as a military move.

Which president was once shot down by enemy antiaircraft batteries?

Distinguished Flying Cross

Naval Lieutenant George H. W. Bush logged 1,228 hours of flight time in his thirty-nine months of service. He was one of four pilots in his fourteen-pilot squadron to survive the war. In September 1944, his Grumman Avenger was shot down by batteries in the Bonin Islands.

Two in the three-man plane died. Bush, who parachuted to safety, was picked up later by a submarine. He was awarded a Distinguished Flying Cross. Fifty years later Bush would commemorate the flight by parachuting from a plane again.

Which president faced enemy gunfire while serving as commander in chief?

Madison and the Militia

President James Madison took command of a military battery manned by Maryland militia trying to repel the invading British marines in 1814 at Bladensburg, Maryland, outside of Washington. Madison was forced to retreat soon thereafter.

Which president's home was named after a famous British admiral?

Lawrence and "Limey"

George Washington's home at Mount Vernon. His older half-brother, Captain Lawrence Washington, who built it with his wife's money (she was a Fairfax), named it after the admiral he had served, Edward Vernon, the victor over the Spanish at Cartagena. Vernon is credited with introducing grog, which was rum laced with lime juice, as a daily ration to prevent scurvy. It caused the nickname of "Limeys" for the English.

Which two presidents served in the same regiment in the Civil War?

Ohio Officers

William McKinley rose from private to major in the Twenty-third Volunteer Ohio Regiment. He served under Rutherford B. Hayes in the same regiment. Hayes rose to the rank of major general.

Who was the only president wounded in the Revolutionary War?

Colonel Monroe

Lieutenant James Monroe was shot in the shoulder in the Battle of Trenton in 1777. For his heroism, he was made a captain. He ended the war as colonel and head of the Virginia Militia. While president, Monroe preferred the title of "Colonel" to "Mr. President."

Which president was blamed for single-handedly starting a major war?

"Crude Colonial"

George Washington was blamed in the London press for igniting the conflict that came to be known in Europe as the Seven Years War and in the Colonies as the French and Indian War. The newspapers characterized him as a "crude colonial." In a scouting expedition to discover the penetration of the French in the Ohio Valley, Major Washington killed a French officer. The French claimed that the officer was an accredited envoy from Montreal. Washington defended himself by asserting that the officer was a spy leading a hostile force.

Which president fudged battle records in order to qualify for a Navy Star?

"Gallant Action"?

Lyndon Johnson joined the Naval Reserve as congressman in 1940. While not resigning his seat, he served briefly in 1942 as a lieutenant commander. On an observation mission to Australia, he reported that his plane was attacked, although the claim was unsupported. For that, General MacArthur awarded Congressman Johnson, "for gallant action," a Silver Star.

Johnson would wear the Silver Star ribbon on his coat the rest of his political career.

Which president, as congressman, led the opposition to the Mexican War?

Spot Check

Abraham Lincoln was the author of "The Spot Resolution," which blamed President James K. Polk for starting the Mexican War. The "spot" referred to a place in Mexican territory where the Whigs claimed that the incident that triggered Polk's war declaration took place. The Democrats argued that it happened within U.S. jurisdiction. Congressman Lincoln did, however, support appropriations for the army during the conflict. Because of his unpopular stand on the war, Whig Lincoln did not seek reelection in 1848.

Which president misrepresented facts to evade the draft?

The Artful Dodger!

Bill Clinton signed a letter of intent in February 1969 to join the Army Reserve and so was removed from the draft pool. He didn't enter the ROTC and didn't inform the draft board either. Later he would thank Colonel Eugene Holmes for "saving [him] from the draft." Clinton said of the war, "The war in Vietnam was a war I opposed and despised."

Who was the first president to order a fleet to sail around the world?

"The Great White Fleet"

Under Theodore Roosevelt, the United States emerged as a new world power in the twentieth century. As assistant secretary of the navy, Roosevelt had championed a bigger navy. In 1907, the navy, called the "Great White Fleet," departed on an around-the-world cruise on the order of the president. An advocate of sea power, Roosevelt began the building of the Panama Canal for faster access to the two oceans that border the United States.

Which president as general turned down any salary?

General Expenses

General George Washington during the Revolutionary War. He did, however, file expense reports that critics claimed were more than his salary would have been.

Which president twice fell off his horse and fainted?

Fainting Frank

Brigadier General Franklin Pierce in the Mexican War. En route to Mexico City, Pierce, while leading troops, fell off his horse twice in the summer of 1847—both times collapsing in a faint. The Whigs, to oppose Pierce's presidential campaign in 1852, tried vainly to make political capital of the story.

The son of which president was shot down in aerial combat?

A Stricken Father

Theodore Roosevelt. His son Quentin, an Army Air Corps pilot, was shot down by German aircraft in 1918. The news devastated his father and some say led to the former president's death six months later.

Which future president won almost five thousand dollars playing poker on a destroyer in World War II?

Lucky Draw?

Richard Nixon. Lieutenant Commander Nixon, to while away his time on a Pacific destroyer away from action, mastered the game of poker. The losers credited their defeats to Nixon's glum poker face. Nixon said it was that he stayed in the game only when he had a good hand. Otherwise he folded.

Which president as general won a historic battle after the war was over?

Postwar Victory

Andrew Jackson. General Jackson won the Battle of New Orleans against the British on January 6, 1815, although the Treaty of Ghent that ended the war had been signed weeks earlier.

Which president, while governor, fled his house when the British Army approached?

Hasty Retreat

Thomas Jefferson fled Monticello in 1779 upon learning that a British unit was approaching. Jefferson's term as governor had technically expired, but he was the "acting governor" until the new one would be installed. Later Jefferson was attacked for what was viewed as a cowardly exit. A committee appointed to review his conduct exonerated him.

Who is the only president to hold the rank of a six-star general?

Generalissimo

George Washington. In 1978 President Jimmy Carter conferred six stars on the first president. He did not believe that General Eisenhower or any other general should outrank the father of our country.

The sons of which two presidents won a Medal of Honor?

Two Heroes

Rutherford B. Hayes and Theodore Roosevelt. Major Webb Hayes in the Spanish American War was awarded a Congressional Medal of Honor for his slipping through enemy lines in the Philippines to gain assistance for his beleaguered force. Brigadier General Theodore Roosevelt Jr., who died of a heart attack on the Normandy Beach, was also awarded a Congressional Medal of Honor posthumously.

Who is the only president to win both a Congressional Medal of Honor and a Nobel Prize for Peace?

Olive Branch as Well as Arrows

President Theodore Roosevelt was given the 1906 Nobel Prize for Peace for settling the Russo-Japanese War in a conference in Portsmouth, New Hampshire, the previous year.

Roosevelt was posthumously awarded the Congressional Medal of Honor, more than a century after his heroic charge leading the Rough Riders up San Juan Hill in July 1898. His regiment unanimously had recommended the award to their commander. President Bill Clinton presented the award posthumously to members of TR's family in the White House in his closing days as president in December 2000.

Which president purchased a substitute for military service during the Civil War?

The Purchase and the Pensions

Grover Cleveland was drafted during the Civil War but chose to purchase a substitute. The twenty-seven-year-old lawyer paid $150 to George Brinski, a Polish immigrant, to take his place. This was a proper legal procedure.

As one who had not fought in the Civil War, Cleveland would display great courage in vetoing hundreds of dubious pension bills for Civil War soldiers. The veterans' lobby, the Grand Army of the Republic, relentlessly attacked him.

Which president carried a handgun on his side while in the White House?

"Big Stick"?

Theodore Roosevelt. The former New York police commissioner, former Dakota Territory deputy sheriff, and colonel of the Rough Riders in Cuba was familiar with guns. He always carried a pistol with him. His most remembered saying as president was: "Speak softly and carry a big stick."

The outspoken TR may not have been known as a soft speaker, but "the damned cowboy in the White House" did carry his "big stick" with him.

NICKNAMES

Which president was called "Father of the American Navy"?

Sailor John

John Adams in 1798 established the Navy Department and appointed the first secretary of the navy. The U.S. Marine Corps was made a permanent branch of the navy, and shipyards were built up and down the East

Coast. Adams's advocacy of the navy predated his presidency. In the Continental Congress in 1777, Adams pushed through legislation that called for the construction of frigates.

Which president was called "the Little Magician"?

Career Pol

Martin Van Buren. This diminutive lawyer of Dutch descent was a career politician who entered the New York State Senate at twenty-nine years of age. The nickname stemmed from his reputation as the political genius behind Andrew Jackson.

Which president was called the "Father of the Constitution"?

"Publius"

James Madison earned the title by drafting much of the document. He was an advocate of a strong central government. Later he marshaled public opinion in the *Federalist Papers* for the Constitution's ratification. His pseudonym for those articles was "Publius."

Which president had the nickname "Tippecanoe"?

"Hard Cider" Harrison

William Henry Harrison defeated the Indians led by Tecumseh in 1800 on the Tippecanoe River, a tributary of the Wabash. The victory over the Shawnees broke the back of their tribal opposition in the Indiana Territory.

In 1840, the Whigs turned to General Harrison over Henry Clay, the leader of the Whigs in Congress, to run against President Van Buren. They made their cry "Tippecanoe and Tyler too." The Whigs packaged Harrison as a log-cabin-born man of the people. Actually, Harrison had a patrician lineage. The son of a signer of the Declaration of Independence, he grew up in Berkley, a mansion in the Virginia tidewater region.

Although it was said that he drank hard cider and not brandy like Van Buren, he grew up with wine on the table, unlike Van Buren.

Which president was known as "Old Rough and Ready"?

The Hero of Buena Vista

Zachary Taylor proved himself as a simple soldier. The tobacco-chewing president had few years of schooling, and his gift for marksmanship led him to seek an army career. Although a disciplinarian, Taylor was affectionately regarded by his troops, who called him "Old Rough and Ready." After his victory at Buena Vista in the Mexican War in 1847, the nickname of America's new hero became known nationwide.

Which president's nickname was "Unconditional Surrender"?

Dictator at Donelson

Ulysses S. Grant went by U.S. Grant when he signed orders. Many of his soldiers thought it might have stood for "Unconditional Surrender." His victory at Fort Donelson in Tennessee in February 1862 was the first major Union victory. In his ultimatum to the Confederate general, Grant stated: "No terms except an unconditional and immediate surrender can be accepted." Afterward he was called "Unconditional Surrender" Grant.

Which president was called "Napoleon of Protection"?

High Tariff Bill

William McKinley. As chairman of the House Ways and Means Committee, he engineered what was called the McKinley Tariff in 1890. The severely protectionist measure increased consumer prices, and McKinley was defeated for reelection to Congress. Undeterred, he returned to Congress in 1894 as champion of the tariff. As the Republican candidate for the presidency in 1896, McKinley made the high tariff and American worker protection his themes.

Which president was called "Old Man Eloquent"?

Outspoken Back Bencher

John Quincy Adams. As a Whig congressman, the former president was outspoken in his attacks against Presidents Jackson and Van Buren. Although his Whig Party was in the minority, he was never deterred in his seventeen years from speaking his mind against slavery, the annexation of Texas, and the Mexican War.

Which president was called "His Accidency"?

Secondhand President

John Tyler was the first vice president to advance to the presidency because of the death of the president. In 1841, Tyler became president following William Harrison, who had the shortest presidency—a little over three weeks.

Disgruntled Whigs who thought Tyler acted more like a Democrat than a Whig called him derisively "His Accidency."

As president, Tyler asked for a new presidential carriage. After inspecting it, Tyler stated: "This is a secondhand carriage." The head of the White House livery reportedly replied: "But aren't you a secondhand president?"

Which president was called "Old Fussbudget"?

A Fussy Bachelor

James Buchanan. The only presidential bachelor was in his midsixties when he became president. Although set in his ways, he was often an indecisive leader. He was particularly fastidious about his clothes, always wearing a spotless black suit and white shirt and white cravat. The term used by his Democratic friends was not unaffectionate.

OCCUPATIONAL
BACKGROUNDS

Who is the only president to have graduated from medical school?

Doc Harrison?

William Henry Harrison studied at the University of Pennsylvania Medical School under the country's most distinguished doctor, Benjamin Rush. Rush, a signer of the Declaration of Independence, was the "father" of mental health and veterinary medicine in America. Rush was a protégé of Benjamin Franklin, and Harrison became a favorite student of his. Harrison, however, would choose the military over medicine as a career.

The American Engineering Society proclaimed that "the two greatest engineers in American history" were Thomas Edison and which president?

The Great Engineer

Herbert Hoover was a mining engineer. This Stanford graduate found coal deposits in China, zinc mines in Australia, silver mines in Burma, and oil deposits in Russia.

Who was the only newspaper publisher to become president?

Press War?

Warren G. Harding was publisher of the *Marion Star* in Ohio and introduced one of the first profit-sharing plans in the newspaper business. Curiously, his Democratic opponent in the 1920 presidential campaign was another publisher, James Cox of the *Dayton Daily News*.

Which president once wrote speeches for Douglas MacArthur?

The General's Ghostwriter

Dwight D. Eisenhower wrote speeches for General Douglas MacArthur— first in the War Department when MacArthur was army chief of staff and then later in the Philippines when MacArthur headed the Filipino Army. When Eisenhower became president, the orator soldier said of Eisenhower: "He was the best clerk I ever had." Eisenhower said this about the general: "Mac had an 'eye' problem—a fatal addiction to the perpendicular pronoun."

Which president was once a fashion model?

Pinup Boy

Gerald Ford, while at Yale Law School, earned extra money as a fashion model. The rugged-looking blond dressed in his naval uniform made the cover of *Cosmopolitan* in 1939.

Which president went from the House of Representatives directly to the White House?

Trifecta

James Garfield. In the election of 1880, Garfield actually qualified for three federal positions at the same time. While serving in the House of Representatives in 1880, Garfield was elected by the legislature of Ohio to serve in the U.S. Senate for the term beginning in March 1881. On November 2, 1880, he was elected president. So Garfield was at the same time president-elect, senator-elect, and member of the House of Representatives.

Who was the only president to have headed a labor union?

Labor of Love

Ronald Reagan headed the Screen Actors Guild in the 1940s. In the aftermath of World War II, Reagan, like Olivia de Havilland and Congressman James Roosevelt, was disturbed by the Communist Party's influence in Hollywood. Reagan rooted out the Communists in the Screen Actors Guild. Because of threats against him, Reagan carried a gun. He did pass to congressional investigators names of actors he believed were Communists, but he opposed the witch-hunting techniques and smears of Congressman Martin Dies and later Senator Joseph McCarthy, which he felt undermined supporters of anti-Communism.

Which president served earlier as governor of the Philippines?

"The Brown Brothers' Big Friend"

William Howard Taft, by appointment of President McKinley, went to Manila in 1900. He converted the Philippines from military to civilian rule, often clashing with General Arthur MacArthur (the father of Douglas). Taft also negotiated with the Vatican for purchase of some 400,000 acres to be distributed to Filipino peasants.

Which president was once police commissioner of New York City?

Top Cop

Theodore Roosevelt was commissioner of the New York City police from 1895 to 1897. He rooted out corruption in the department and would make night tours incognito to catch corrupt police officers. Once when coming from a ball, the police commissioner, carrying a billy club and dressed in white tie and top hat, apprehended a criminal.

Which president was rejected by the FBI after graduating from law school?

G-Man Dick?

Richard Nixon. After Duke Law School, Nixon applied for a position with the FBI and was turned down. J. Edgar Hoover later said it was because in 1937 the Bureau was in the midst of the Depression and had an overload of applications.

Which president had his license to practice law suspended?

"Slick Willy"

Bill Clinton was informed by the Arkansas State Bar Review that his license was suspended because of his sworn misrepresentation in the Paula Jones civil case in Arkansas.

PERSONAL ACHIEVEMENTS

Who was the only president to be granted a patent for an invention?

A Patent Success

Abraham Lincoln received a patent in 1849 for his invention of adjustable buoyant chambers for steamboats. This device enabled large ships to navigate in shallow waters, including canals. As one who lived all his life in the area of the Mississippi River and its tributaries, Lincoln had witnessed all the labor and time it took to transfer loads from larger to smaller crafts. His adjustable chamber allowed boats to alter their draft in water.

Which president established the forerunner relief organizations that eventually became CARE and UNICEF?

Humanitarian Hoover

Herbert Hoover, in the First World War, established the American Relief Committee in 1914. Then he headed its successor, the American Relief Commission, which administered after that war thirty-four million tons of food, clothing, and supplies valued at $5.2 billion. This relief organization was later adopted by the League of Nations and then the United Nations.

Which president was conversant in four languages?

The Gift of Tongues

John Quincy Adams grew up a diplomat's son. His formative years were spent in Paris and Amsterdam. By the time he entered Harvard, he was conversant in French, Dutch, and Spanish, not to mention his knowledge of Latin and Greek.

He later served as minister to the Netherlands and then Prussia. In Prussia, he picked up German. Later he went to Russia; however, he did not master the language of that country.

Of his term as secretary of state under James Monroe, it can be said that no secretary of state before or since John Quincy Adams ever possessed such a wide command of languages.

Who is the only president to have been an Eagle Scout?

A Good Scout

Gerald Ford, as a fourteen-year-old in Grand Rapids, Michigan, in Troop 14 earned the coveted youth award. In the ranks of famous Eagle Scouts, he was later joined by such notables as astronaut and senator John Glenn and home-run king Hank Aaron.

Which president invented a letter-copying press?

Polymath President

Thomas Jefferson—lawyer, architect, philosopher, author, musician, equestrian, and wine vintner/connoisseur—was also an inventor. In addition to the letter-copying device that enabled him to keep a file of the letters he wrote, he invented a swivel chair, a new plow, and a pedometer.

Which president foreshadowed his early debating talent when at the age of ten he won the debate proposition: "Resolved: Insects are beneficial to mankind"?

To "Bee" or Not to "Bee"

Richard Nixon took the unpopular side of this sixth-grade debate because he figured it would better display his skill. Without bees, he argued, there would be no pollination. Starvation, he propounded, could be the result.

Which president explored the Amazon River?

A "Natural" Naturalist

Theodore Roosevelt, at the age of nine, wrote and published a paper: "The Natural History of Insects." As a boy, he was a fledgling zoologist and established his own "Roosevelt Natural Museum of History" in his house, snaring countless creatures, big and small, and preserving and cataloging their carcasses. At Harvard, he headed the Natural History Club and lectured the Nuthall Ornithological Club on rare birds he had seen.

After he was president, Roosevelt went on an exploration trip down the Amazon River in Brazil. Later he went on safari treks in Africa.

It was his first wife, Alice Lee, who talked him out of pursuing a career as a zoologist when he left Harvard.

Which president wrote a constitution that remains the oldest written governmental charter in the world?

Conventional Wisdom

John Adams. For the Massachusetts convention in 1780, Adams drafted the state constitution of Massachusetts that, though amended like the U.S. Constitution, remains essentially the same document today.

A plaque honors which president for saving seventy-seven lives?

Rescuer Ron

In Dixon, Illinois, there is a plaque at the Lowell Park riverside honoring lifeguard Ronald Reagan, who in the summers from 1927 to 1932 rescued seventy-seven swimmers from drowning. The plaque was erected before he earned fame as movie actor and later governor and then president.

Who was the only president to be a thirty-third-degree Mason?

Highest-Degree Harry

Harry Truman. In the Masonic Order, thirty-two degrees is the highest level to which one can accede. The thirty-third is awarded only to those of eminent character and accomplishments. George Washington, the most famous Mason, was only a thirty-two-degree Mason.

The story is told that a Baptist neighbor of Truman, who was also a fellow Masonic Lodge member, was chided by a visitor for having a picture of Pope Pius XII in his den. "No," said the neighbor, "don't you recognize him. It's Harry Truman in his Masonic regalia."

Other presidents who were Masons include George Washington, James Monroe, Andrew Jackson, James Polk, James Buchanan, Andrew Johnson, James Garfield, William McKinley, Theodore Roosevelt, William Howard Taft, Warren Harding, Franklin Roosevelt, Lyndon Johnson, and Gerald Ford.

One president was once elected wearing the Anti-Mason Party label. John Quincy Adams after he was president was elected to Congress as an Anti-Mason. Later he switched to the Whig Party.

Which president wrote the parliamentary rules manual that is still in use in the U.S. Senate today?

Jefferson Rules

As vice president under John Adams, Jefferson found himself with time on his hands. During that time, he wrote a procedure for the U.S. Senate. *A Manual of Parliamentary Practice* was published in 1801. Senator Robert Byrd of West Virginia, the Senate's master of parliamentary procedures, calls it his "bible."

Which president, as a deputy sheriff in the West, arrested two outlaws?

Man in the White Hat

As deputy sheriff of Billings County in the Dakota Territory, Theodore Roosevelt arrested two cattle-rustling outlaws. Roosevelt was a rancher in the territory at that time.

PERSONAL STYLE

Which president deliberately copied the style of dress and attire of a previous president?

Copycat

James Monroe was a tall, husky, reddish-haired Virginian. He was flattered when people told him he resembled General Washington. He was also proud that he shared the distinction with the general of being the only other president to have fought in the Revolutionary War. Unlike Jefferson or Madison, Monroe chose the blue tunic, tan waistcoat, and white stockings of his hero—even though by 1816 they had long gone out of style.

One president favored tailor-made suits from London. He never carried a wallet or change because of the bulge it would have made in his suits. Who was he?

Savile Row President

John F. Kennedy began wearing tailor-made suits from Savile Row in London, when his father served as ambassador to the Court of St. James in the late 1930s. His made-to-order shirts came from Jermyn Street. He detested the button-down shirts of Brooks Brothers.

Which president had more than two hundred pairs of trousers in his closet?

Prince Arthur

Chester Alan Arthur was nicknamed "the Elegant Arthur" for his extensive wardrobe. Sturdily built, the handsome and tall Arthur developed a taste for fine food and wine. He was the most urbane of the nineteenth-century presidents.

Whether the occasion called for formal, business, country, or sporting attire, Arthur was impeccably dressed.

Which president wore the same hat every day?

Old Hat

The bald John Quincy Adams wore the same hat for ten years. Adams was known for being notoriously careless about his appearance.

Which president wore a red carnation in his lapel every day?

Brighten up the Day

Because it pleased his wife, William McKinley wore a fresh red carnation in his lapel every day. He also would sport a spotless white vest, which he would change two or three times a day.

Which president, while visiting cities, would stop his carriage outside the town and don fresh attire that would be immaculate for the occasion?

Gentleman George

George Washington was meticulous about his appearance. He would powder his wig, brush his tunic, and polish his boots more than once a day. When traveling, he would keep a fresh set of attire in the carriage and change before arriving in the town where he was to make an appearance.

Who was the first president not to wear a hat?

Hat Ban?

John F. Kennedy hated hats. As president, he also thought it distinguished him from his predecessor, the bald General Eisenhower, who always wore a homburg. As a contrast to the seventy-year-old former president, JFK wanted to advertise his youth. His refusal to wear hats caused a fashion trend. Danbury, Connecticut, the nation's hat capital, which voted handsomely for Kennedy, found itself in an economic slump.

Which president consistently wore a stovepipe hat and shawl in public appearances?

A Long Drink of Water

The six-foot, four-inch Abraham Lincoln, though not a vain man, took pride in his height. The big crown of the stovepipe hat and the long shawl that draped down his chest enhanced his stature. This sartorial style of Lincoln was first noted in his debates with the short and stubby Senator Stephen Douglas in 1858.

Which president often wore as chief executive clothes he had made himself?

Tailor-Made

Andrew Johnson was a self-made man with no formal education. He started out as an apprentice to a tailor and later opened his own shop. He rose to be governor of Tennessee. While governor, he made his own suit for his inauguration as vice president in 1865.

Pets and Animals

Which president loved his dog so much that he had a photograph taken of the dog to keep by him at the White House?

Family Portrait

Abraham Lincoln. Lincoln was distraught when he was advised that his ten-year-old terrier, Skippy, might not survive the long train trip to Washington in 1861. So he had a photograph taken of Skippy—one of the first canine portraits by camera.

Which president kept a lion and bear cub in the White House?

Teddy Bear

Theodore Roosevelt. Roosevelt, who once considered a career as a zoologist, loved animals. As a boy, he kept embalmed dead animals in his own home natural museum. His love of big-game hunting was not the shooting but the stalking and working of animals in the wild.

His rescuing of a bear cub in Mississippi led to the creation of the most popular stuffed animal in history—the "teddy bear." Clifford Berryman, a political cartoonist for the *Washington Star*, penned a little cub as a mascot for TR in his sketches. Soon a doll manufacturer was making teddy bears. National Teddy Bear Day is celebrated every year on TR's birthday, October 27.

Which president kept a mockingbird in his White House office?

Mocking Presence

Thomas Jefferson loved this small brown bird he brought from Monticello with him. He was amused by the bird's imitation of the robin's chirp and the blue jay's warble.

Which president so loved his old horse that he buried the horse in the back lawn of his house and put up a gravestone?

Horse Sense

John Tyler. Tyler loved his old roan, "The General." He had a grave dug behind his house, Sherwood Forest, near Richmond. The gravestone over the grave read:

> Here lies the body of my good horse, "The General." For twenty years he bore me around the circuit of my practice and in all that time, he never made a blunder. Would that his master could say the same!
>
> JOHN TYLER

Which presidential dog "wrote" a number of books, including a bestseller?

Millie the Mommy

Millie Bush. The liver-spotted springer spaniel authored, with the help of first lady Barbara Bush, books about her dog's life in the White House. The royalties went to a fund to combat illiteracy.

"First dog" Millie had a son named Ranger.

Mrs. Bush, in telling friends of the defeat in 1992, said that George bore up well with the loss, but then weeks later his favorite uncle, George Walker, died and then his mother. He broke up, however, with the death of Ranger. "Now Ranger is gone too," said the president, with tears filling his eyes.

Which president sent a destroyer to pick up his dog?

Fala

Franklin Delano Roosevelt. The president's little Scottie was named Fala. In a trip to Alaska in 1944, Roosevelt's dog was mistakenly left behind. The navy did pick him up because it was due to their negligence that he didn't make the boat. Republicans in the presidential campaign attacked Roosevelt, who with his wit devastatingly turned the incident to his advantage. He said:

> These Republicans—not content are they to attack me, my wife Eleanor, or my sons, Jimmy and Elliott. They now attack my little dog Fala. The Republican fiction writers allege that an American destroyer was sent to Alaska, and I can say that Fala, with every drop of his Scottish blood, resents their base attack. . . .

The Secret Service called Fala "The Informer" because on unannounced and unscheduled trips, the sight of Fala, when let out to do his business, signaled the nearby presence of Roosevelt.

Sardar was the name of the Arabian horse given by the president of Pakistan to which first lady?

"Never Look a Gift Horse . . ."

Jacqueline Bouvier Kennedy. In 1962, President Mohammed Ayub Khan sent an Arabian stallion—a prized racing horse whose bloodlines boasted centuries of selective breeding—as a gift. Sardar was stabled at the Kennedy farm in Virginia. Mrs. Kennedy was an accomplished equestrian and often rode in hunts in Virginia and later in New Jersey, where Sardar lived out his last years.

A famous address by one future president is called by his dog's name. Who was the president?

The "Checkers" Speech

Richard Nixon. Taking a cue from Roosevelt's use of Fala, Nixon closed his defense of a "secret" expense fund with this reference to the family cocker spaniel, Checkers:

> One other thing I probably should tell you, because if I don't they'll probably be saying this about me too. We did get something, a gift, after the election. A man down in Texas heard Pat on the radio mention the fact that our two youngsters would like to have a dog. And, believe it or not, the day before we left on this campaign trip we got a message from Union Station in Baltimore saying they had a package for us. We went down to get it. You know what it was? It was a little cocker spaniel dog in a crate that he sent all the way from Texas. Black and white spotted. And our little girl Tricia, the six-year-old, named it Checkers. And you know, the kids love the dog, and I just want to say this right now, that regardless of what they say about it, we're gonna keep it.

Which president is credited as "the Father of the American mule"?

"Royal Gift"

George Washington. Washington was a serious and successful farmer. His careful administration of his estate made his holdings worth more than half a million dollars at his death. Animal husbandry was one of his keenest interests. He promoted the use of mules—the offspring of a mare and a donkey—in America. He wrote to the king of Spain, who bred the best donkeys in the world. King Carlos sent him a prize donkey, which Washington called Royal Gift. The first attempts of mating were fruitless.

In a letter to Lafayette, Washington commented:

> The Jack I have already received from Spain in appearance is fine, but his late Royal master, tho' past his grand climacteric, cannot be less moved by female allurements than he is; or when prompted can proceed with more deliberation and majestic solemnity to the matter of procreation.

The German shepherd of which presidential family bit the visiting Canadian prime minister?

Dog's Meat?

Franklin Delano Roosevelt's dog, Rex, the German shepherd, took a chunk from the thigh of Mackenzie King, the Canadian prime minister, when King was visiting the Roosevelt home in Hyde Park in 1941. The canine snarl and bite of King happily did not prevent the issuance of the Hyde Park Agreement, a declaration of common defense in time of war.

Jeff Davis was the name of the favorite horse of which president?

"Whoa Jeff!"

Ulysses S. Grant. General Grant's favorite horse was named Jeff Davis after the president of the Confederacy. The name that Grant gave to this brown gelding in honor of his foe reveals a puckish humor in Grant.

Which president, while still in office, once rode on horseback for a total of a hundred miles?

Dawn to Dusk

Theodore Roosevelt. In late February 1908, the fifty-one-year-old president rode from New York to Albany—sunrise to sunset. He did this when he was told that the test for Army cavalrymen was twenty-five miles a day. He belittled that standard, saying he could do a hundred. He used three horses for close to a hundred miles. TR, a fanatic for physical fitness, wanted to test himself and establish some sort of record for presidential stamina.

One White House dog almost caused its owner to be shot by onrushing Secret Service agents. Who was the president?

"Give Me Liberty, or Give Me Death"?

Gerald Ford. In 1975, Liberty, the retriever living in the Ford White House, awakened the president in response to a call of nature. Ford took the dog down the elevator from the second floor and let Liberty and himself out the Oval Office to do his business. Ford and his dog, in the guarded periphery of the White House, set off the alarm. Secret Servicemen armed with guns approached "the intruder," who was the president.

Which presidential family had a raccoon in the White House as their pet?

Rebecca the Raccoon

The Coolidges. Actually, it was Grace Coolidge's special friend. She called it Rebecca. Mrs. Coolidge once took it with her to a school for deaf-mutes in Washington.

Which president let sheep graze on the White House lawn?

"Sheepish" Conduct

Woodrow Wilson. During World War I, the demand for food, especially meat, ran high. New recruits had left farms. But more important, the ravages of war in Europe had caused close to a million refugees, some of whom were close to starvation. As an example to the country, Wilson announced that sheep would graze the White House lawn.

Which White House family kept a parrot as a pet?

Patriotic Parrot

The Madisons. It was the favorite of the inimitable Dolley Madison. It would announce to guests: "Constitution . . . Constitution," which, of course, her husband, James, had helped draft.

Which president let the White House lawn serve as a pasture for his cow?

Bovine Boon

William Howard Taft. His Guernsey dairy cow, Goldie, was both a pet and a provider of milk in the Taft tenure at the White House.

PHYSICAL
FEATURES

***Which president tipped the scales at more than three hundred
pounds?***

A Whale of a Guy

The walrus-mustached William Howard Taft was whalelike in size. At
five feet, eleven inches, Taft was 210 pounds when he graduated from
Yale in 1878. When he entered the White House, he weighed 320 pounds.

The presidency was not an office he enjoyed. His wife, Helen Herron Taft, had propelled him toward it. At the White House, his weight
climbed to 345. Taft was a trencherman. A White House breakfast would
include eggs, sausage, bacon, and even pancakes.

He was good-natured about his weight. Once Chauncey Depew
pointed to Taft's massive tummy and said: "What are you going to name
the baby?"

Taft said: "If it's a boy, he will be a junior. If it's a girl, I'll name it
after her mother—but if, as I suspect, it is only gas, I'll name it Chauncey
Depew."

Once, when the Tafts were vacationing in Florida, Mrs. Taft said to
their sons Robert and Charles: "Why don't you go out and swim?"

The boys replied: "We can't. Daddy is in the Atlantic."

When Taft was governor of the Philippines, he reported in a dispatch that he had reached an inland post after a ride of fifty miles. Secretary of State Elihu Root cabled him: "How's the horse?"

Who was the first president to wear a beard?

Bedell's Beard

Abraham Lincoln did not grow his famous beard until after he was nominated for the presidency in 1860. He had been clean-shaven, but during his campaign, he received a letter from a little girl named Grace Bedell, who lived in Westfield, New York. She wrote that she had seen his portrait and thought he would look better with whiskers. She promised that if he let his whiskers grow, she would try to persuade her older brothers, who were Democrats, to vote for him.

Lincoln wrote back to her on October 19, 1860:

My Dear Little Miss:

Your very agreeable letter of the fifteenth is received. I regret the necessity of saying that I have no daughter. I have three sons: one seventeen, one nine, and one seven years of age. They, with their mother, constitute my whole family. As to the whiskers, having never worn any, do you not think people would call it a piece of silly affectation if I should begin it now?

Your very sincere well-wisher,

A. Lincoln

Lincoln, however, soon changed his mind on the subject. When he was on his way to Washington to be inaugurated, the train stopped at Westfield. Remembering young Grace Bedell, Lincoln inquired after her. It was soon discovered that she was present in the crowd. The president-elect asked her to come forward so she might see that he had allowed his whiskers to grow at her request. She timidly obliged, and he lifted her up and kissed her while the crowd roared its approval. He wore a beard ever after.

Who were the only two presidents in the twentieth century to have facial hair?

Are Mustaches a Mistake?

Theodore Roosevelt and his hand-picked successor for president, William Howard Taft. Roosevelt flashed a bristly mustache under his pince-nez glasses. Taft's upper lip looked more like a walrus. The mustached governor of New York, Tom Dewey, ran for the presidency twice—in 1944 and 1948—but lost.

After his close defeat in his run for the presidency, former Vice President Al Gore grew a beard. He shaved it off in 2002 as he prepared himself for another presidential race.

Abraham Lincoln was the tallest president at six feet, four inches.
Who was the second tallest at six feet, three and one-half inches?

The Tallest Tree in the Forest

Lyndon Johnson, at six feet, three and one-half inches, always claimed
to be. In addition, George Washington's secretary, Tobias Lear, measured
Washington in his funeral bier at six feet, three and one-half inches—a
virtual giant in the eighteenth century.

Which president weighed less than one hundred pounds?

"Little Jemmy"

At barely five feet, three inches, James Madison weighed just more than a hundred pounds with clothes and boots. Washington Irving described Madison as "a withered little apple-john." His nickname, "Little Jemmy," emphasizes both his small stature and his puppy dog loyalty to Thomas Jefferson.

Which president spoke with a distinct lisp?

"My Name Is Adamth"?

In 1781, John Adams, while minister to the Netherlands, contracted a severe fever. After that, pyorrhea began to eat away his teeth. He refused to wear dentures, and so he talked with a lisp.

Which president had pockmarks on his face because of smallpox he had contracted in his youth?

"The Pits"

George Washington, as an eighteen-year-old, went to Barbados. It was his only visit outside the thirteen colonies or states. There he incurred smallpox. The results were disfiguring marks. His bout with smallpox, however, immunized him in the Revolutionary War, when the disease ravaged his Continental Army.

Which president had walrus ivories for his false teeth?

Wooden or Walrus?

By age fifty-seven, when George Washington took his inaugural oath as president, he had lost most of his teeth. Contrary to popular belief, he did not have wooden false teeth. He had made for him the top-of-the-line dentures fashioned from the ivory of walrus tusks.

The teeth were uncomfortable, which accounts for Gilbert Stuart's pinched-mouth portrait that is on the dollar bill. The family preferred Charles Wilson Peale's portrait of the general.

Which president said, when a handsome portrait of himself was presented to him at the White House: "I presume in painting this beautiful portrait you took your idea from my principles not my person"?

Principles of Pulchritude

Abraham Lincoln said that to Edwin Marchant, the artist who had painted the portrait on a commission by the Union League in Philadelphia. Marchant had stayed at the White House for months working on the portrait. The painting imparted a measure of nobility to Lincoln's homely features.

POLITICAL POTPOURRI

Who was the last president to serve with no former presidents alive?

All Alone

Richard Nixon. In 1973, Harry Truman and Lyndon Johnson died. Nixon was the only one whom someone could address as "Mr. President."

Herbert Hoover was also all alone when Calvin Coolidge died in January 1933, two months before Franklin Delano Roosevelt would be sworn in.

Ulysses S. Grant, when Andrew Johnson died in 1875, was also all alone. Millard Fillmore had died the year before.

Which president, as a legislator, jumped out of a State House window just before a vote was called?

The Lincoln Leap

In 1836, the Democratic-controlled Illinois state legislature would not raise the revenue to enable the state to redeem its bonds. The Democrats wanted to embarrass the banks and their Whig friends in the business community. Under state law, default would be incurred if the legislature adjourned without action.

The minority party Whigs, led by Lincoln, tried to prevent adjournment by denying the quorum necessary to vote for adjournment. On one fateful afternoon, the Democratic speaker, who was presiding while Lincoln was addressing the House, realized that the presence of Lincoln and a few of his fellow Whigs constituted a quorum. He quickly had a vote for adjournment called.

Lincoln sensed the situation and leaped out of the State House window.

In their first year in Congress, these two men engaged in a formal debate on labor union reform. They would later be elected presidents. Who were they?

The First Nixon-Kennedy Debate

In a foreshadowing of the Nixon-Kennedy debate on television in the 1960 presidential campaign, the same two men, as congressmen, debated the Taft-Hartley Bill in 1947 in McKeesport, Pennsylvania (near Pittsburgh). The two congressmen shared a sleeping car and traveled to McKeesport. Nixon was for the bill and Kennedy against the bill, which was later passed by the Eightieth Congress. The debate was later carried on local radio.

Which president in state duties and ceremonies met Winston Churchill, Charles de Gaulle, Chiang Kai-shek, Mao Tse-tung, Chou En-lai, Golda Meir, Fidel Castro, Ho Chi Minh, Nikita Khrushchev, Leonid Brezhnev, Anwar Sadat, Reza Shah Pahlevi, Jawaharlal Nehru, and Konrad Adenauer?

Peripatetic President

Richard Nixon, as vice president under Eisenhower and then as president met these world leaders. Churchill and de Gaulle were the two giants he most revered. Nixon also developed great respect for Chou En-lai, Anwar Sadat, and Golda Meir.

Which president built the Treasury Building to exclude his view of the Capitol?

Capitol Blackout

President Andrew Jackson's relations with Congress were particularly acrimonious. He especially despised Henry Clay, the leader of the Whig opposition. Accordingly, Jackson had the new Treasury Building situated right on Pennsylvania Avenue just east of the White House. After it was erected, Jackson bragged: "Now I can't see the Capitol any more."

Which president actually drafted the Monroe Doctrine?

Ambitious Adams

John Quincy Adams. As secretary of state, he drafted the doctrine. Actually, the barring of European meddling in South America was first suggested by the British minister George Canning. The doctrine was originally supposed to be a joint declaration, but because of the dispute with the British over the Oregon Territory, James Monroe wanted it to be a solely American doctrine. Adams, however, saw it as a vehicle for his own ambitions to succeed Monroe as president.

Which future Democratic president was a key witness in defending a former Republican president on libel charges?

No Day of Infamy

Franklin Delano Roosevelt. In 1916, former President Theodore Roosevelt was sued for libel by the Republican state chairman of New York. George Barnes denied TR's charge that Republican Barnes was in collusion with Tammany Hall, the New York City Democratic machine.

FDR, then assistant secretary of the navy under Woodrow Wilson, was a former Democratic state senator. His testimony was conclusive. Every Democrat knew, FDR had stated, that Barnes was linked to the Democratic machine.

Which president had slum villages named for him?

"Hoovervilles"

Herbert Hoover. "Hooverville" was the name given to shantytowns in the Depression; the label was heartbreaking for Hoover. Interestingly, in World War I, "Hoover" was used as a verb. "Hooverize" meant to economize on food—to voluntarily ration. Hoover, as U.S. food administrator, urged Americans to observe "wheatless and meatless days."

The cabinet of which president resigned in protest to his veto of a bill?

Cabinet Exodus

John Tyler. In 1841, Tyler's cabinet resigned to protest his veto of a bill creating the Fiscal Corporation of the United States, which would collect and disburse U.S. revenues.

Which president appeared on the cover of Time *magazine fifty-four times?*

Cover Boy

Richard Nixon. In the Nixon Museum and Library in Yorba Linda, California, one wall features the fifty-four *Time* magazine covers. It is evidence of his long span in public life dating from the Alger Hiss case in 1947 to his visit with Premier Yeltsin just before his death in 1994.

Which president segregated the U.S. military forces?

Southern Segregationist?

Woodrow Wilson made segregation in the military a matter of official policy. Before Wilson, there had been black units, but his official policy required segregated housing. Separate public accommodations in Washington, D.C., were also put in place under Wilson. Wilson, a southerner by birth, was a segregationist. No blacks were invited to the White House during his administration. He once told a black audience: "Segregation is not humiliating but a benefit and ought to be regarded by you gentlemen."

Who was the first president to be the subject of a serious impeachment attempt?

Tyler in a Tight Spot

John Tyler. In 1843, a congressman from Tyler's home state of Virginia introduced an impeachment resolution with charges of corruption, misconduct in office, high crimes, and misdemeanors. The motion was defeated with 83 ayes to 127 nays.

Which president anonymously wrote legislation for states that would annul or "veto" federal statutes?

Virginian Veto

Thomas Jefferson. While vice president under John Adams, Jefferson drafted the Virginia and Kentucky Resolutions in 1798, which would override national legislation. Jefferson did it anonymously. Not until after he left the presidency did the fact of his authorship leak out.

Who was the first president to engage a speechwriter?

Washington Writers

George Washington. He used the services of Jefferson and Madison but mostly Alexander Hamilton, who drafted his farewell address.

Washington was following the practice of eighteenth-century English monarchs whose speeches to Parliament were written by the prime minister.

The presidents who never used speechwriters include John Adams, Thomas Jefferson, James Madison, John Quincy Adams, Abraham Lincoln, Grover Cleveland, Theodore Roosevelt, and Woodrow Wilson.

Which president once accused Benjamin Franklin of being a British spy?

Madison Madness?

James Madison. In 1775, the twenty-four-year-old Madison wrote to a Princeton College friend in Philadelphia, Pennsylvania, William Bradford, that he believed Benjamin Franklin, who was representing some of the colonies' interests in London, had secret ties to the monarchy. Franklin, he said, must be disloyal if he was not an active informer. "Suspicion of his guilt amounts very nearly to a proof of its reality."

PRESIDENTIAL
APPOINTMENTS

Which president appointed as his secretary of state a man whose grandfather also had served as secretary of state?

Foster Care

Dwight D. Eisenhower appointed John Foster Dulles as his secretary of state. His grandfather, John Foster, had been secretary of state under Benjamin Harrison. Interestingly, Dulles's uncle, Robert Lansing, had also been secretary of state serving Woodrow Wilson.

Dulles's father had died young, and John Foster Dulles, his brother, Allen, and sister, Eleanor, were partially raised by the grandfather John Foster. Allen Dulles became the first director of the CIA. Considered the brightest of the children by many, Eleanor Dulles headed the German desk at the State Department.

Which president appointed his brother to the cabinet?

Brotherly Love

John F. Kennedy made his younger brother Robert attorney general. The thirty-five-year-old Kennedy's previous legal experience was as a counsel for a Senate committee. Subsequent legislation now forbids the

appointment of members of the immediate family. JFK disarmingly said: "I think Bobby needs some experience in the law."

Which president's administration had four secretaries of state?

State of Flux?

Harry Truman. Truman inherited Edward Stettinius, FDR's last secretary of state. Truman soon appointed James Byrnes, whom he chose in part because the secretary of state was next in line at that time to succeed him. Truman preferred someone who had elected experience. It was an uneasy relationship (Byrnes thought he should have been picked instead of Truman to be vice president under Roosevelt in 1944). Truman then chose General George C. Marshall, who would formulate the Marshall Plan. Truman, however, was the closest to Dean Acheson, who became secretary of state in 1949.

Which president appointed his wife to head a presidential commission?

Hillary on Health

President Bill Clinton appointed first lady Hillary Rodham Clinton to head a commission on Medicare. The legislation emanating from that commission was defeated in the House.

Who was the first president to appoint a woman to the Supreme Court?

Sandra the Supreme

Ronald Reagan appointed Sandra Day O'Connor in 1981. She had been a judge on the Arizona Court of Appeals. A former Republican state senator, O'Connor was approved ninety-nine to zero. Interestingly, while at Stanford Law School, she once dated Associate Justice William Rehnquist, who was later made Chief Justice by Reagan in 1986.

Which president appointed the first African American to serve as executive assistant to the president?

First Black in the White House

Dwight D. Eisenhower. Frederick Morrow served in the White House eight years in the role of adviser on civil rights.

Who was the first president to appoint a woman to the cabinet?

Frances the First

FDR. He made Frances Perkins secretary of labor in 1933. She played a key role in the establishment of the Social Security System in New York state in 1935. She had served with Governor Roosevelt in Albany, New York.

The father served as secretary of agriculture for a Republican president. The son served in the same post for a Democratic president. Who were the two presidents?

Farmer Father and Son

Henry A. Wallace Sr. served under Presidents Harding and Coolidge. His son, Henry Wallace Jr., was Franklin Delano Roosevelt's secretary of agriculture and was elected vice president in 1940. Wallace would run for president in 1948 on the Progressive Party ticket against Truman; he opposed the cold war with Russia.

The Wallaces in Iowa had pioneered a hybrid corn and produced a magazine, *Wallaces' Farmer*.

Who was the first president to appoint a Catholic to the Supreme Court?

The "Dred" Decision

Andrew Jackson appointed Roger Taney of Maryland as Chief Justice in 1836. The Maryland Catholic served until 1864. He was the author of the Dred Scott Decision in 1857, which treated fugitive slaves as stolen or missing property. Taney had formerly served Jackson as secretary of the treasury.

Next to John Marshall, whom he succeeded, Taney was the longest-presiding Chief Justice.

Who was the first president to appoint a person of the Jewish faith to the Supreme Court?

Barrister Brandeis

Woodrow Wilson appointed Lewis Brandeis in 1916. Brandeis served thirty years on the Court and was the author of "The Brandeis Brief," which wielded economic statistics to unseat legal precedents. He called himself "the people's advocate."

Which president appointed the first Jewish envoy?

Mordecai the Minister

James Madison appointed Mordecai Manuel Noah as United States consul to Tunis in 1813. He was the first American diplomat of the Jewish faith.

Who was the first president to appoint an African American to the cabinet?

Housing Head

Lyndon Johnson appointed Robert C. Weaver to be secretary of housing and urban development in 1966. The department had been established as part of Johnson's Great Society program.

Who was the only president to retain the entire cabinet throughout his presidency?

Clean Slate

Franklin Pierce, in his four years from 1853 to 1857, had no dismissals, no resignations, and no deaths in his cabinet.

Who was the first president to appoint African Americans to federal positions?

"Black Man's Buddy"

Theodore Roosevelt appointed many in his term, including postmasters in Mississippi and collectors in South Carolina. The appointments triggered a storm of criticism in the South. Roosevelt insisted he was choosing on merit only. His friend Booker T. Washington helped him create a slate of qualified African Americans. Roosevelt was called the "Black Man's Buddy" and worse.

Who was the first president to appoint a Hispanic to the cabinet.

Olé!

President George H. W. Bush appointed Manuel Luhan of New Mexico to be secretary of the interior in 1989.

Which president was the first to appoint a person of the Jewish faith to a cabinet office?

Oscar Winner

Theodore Roosevelt appointed Oscar S. Straus to be secretary of commerce and labor. A German immigrant, Straus had served as ambassador to Turkey under President McKinley.

Which president appointed the nephew of a living former president to the Supreme Court?

Brainy Bushrod

John Adams appointed in 1798 Bushrod Washington, a nephew of General Washington, to the Supreme Court. An original member of the Phi Beta Kappa's first chapter at William and Mary, Bushrod later was the executor of his uncle's estate.

Which president appointed Robert Lincoln, the son of the martyred president, to be secretary of war?

Secretary Lincoln

James Garfield in 1881 appointed the oldest and only surviving son of Abraham Lincoln. In 1885, Robert Lincoln served under President Arthur as minister to Britain. Later he would be president of the Pullman Company. Robert's grandson, who died in 1987, was the last surviving descendant of Lincoln.

Which president appointed a thirty-one-year-old to a major cabinet office?

"Youth Will Be Served"

George Washington appointed Alexander Hamilton to be secretary of treasury. The first president has the distinction of appointing the youngest cabinet. Jefferson, as secretary of state at the age of forty-five, was among the oldest of Washington's appointments. His attorney general Edward Randolph was only thirty-six. His secretary of war, Henry Knox, was thirty-eight. (Fort Knox was named after him.)

PUBLIC OFFICES HELD

Which president was elected senator after he was president?

Acquitted Andy

Andrew Johnson. The impeached but acquitted president was elected senator in 1875. He left the White House in 1869 and did not attend the inauguration of his successor, General Grant, but returned to Greeneville, Tennessee, where he was given a hero's welcome.

Johnson made only one speech as senator in which he denounced Grant's Reconstruction policy.

Which president presided over the Constitutional Convention?

Let George Do It

George Washington. If General Washington had not consented to preside over the gathering assembly of delegates in Philadelphia, it would have been considered a "rump convention," an illegal, perhaps subversive, assembly. The Articles of Confederation were still the structure of the constituted government. Washington's name and towering prestige gave the convention the stamp of authority. Although Washington said few words, what he did say at the beginning set the tone: "Let us raise a standard to which the wise and honest can repair."

On another occasion, the old soldier stepped down from the chair to give his view on a proposal to establish a standing army of three thousand men. "I suppose we should entertain another provision that no foreign army of more than three thousand men should be allowed to invade the continental United States."

Who was the only president who also served as Speaker of the House?

"Thou Shalt Not Covet Thy Neighbor's House"

James K. Polk was Speaker of the House. The Democratic congressman from Tennessee was Speaker from 1835 to 1839, six years before he was sworn in as president.

Polk defeated Senator Henry Clay in 1844. The Whig Clay, however, had three times served as Speaker of the House. Clay ran unsuccessfully three times for the presidency. Clay said once: "I'd rather be right than president." Perhaps he got his wish.

When the Kentuckian heard that the lesser known Polk from the neighboring state of Tennessee was to be his opponent, Clay shook his head. "It will be easy," said a fellow Whig. Clay replied: "No, it will be harder. I need him as an opponent like a 'polk' in the head."

Who was the only president to also serve as chief justice?

"The Justice in Fair Round Belly"

Former President William Howard Taft was appointed chief justice of the Supreme Court by President Harding in 1921. Then a professor at Yale, Taft finally had the office he had always sought. Three times Taft had turned down Theodore Roosevelt's offer to move him to the highest court—first in 1902, because Taft felt he had work to finish as governor of the Philippines. Then, as secretary of war, he twice rejected the court offer because of pressing emergencies in the world.

It is widely believed that his wife, who had always wanted the White House for her husband, played the decisive role in his rejections of the court appointment before 1908. The three-hundred-pound Taft presiding over the Supreme Court calls to memory the Shakespeare phrase: "the justice in fair round belly."

Which presidents served as secretary of state before assuming the presidency?

Prime Minister

Thomas Jefferson, James Madison, James Monroe, John Quincy Adams, Martin Van Buren, and James Buchanan. The cabinet position was the first created and is first in precedence. It is the premier ministry.

It should also be mentioned that William Howard Taft served as acting secretary of state during an illness of Elihu Root in the presidency of Theodore Roosevelt.

Which president served as a congressman after he was president?

The Gentleman from Massachusetts

John Quincy Adams left the White House in 1829, but he returned the next year as a congressman from Massachusetts. As a member of the Anti-Mason Party, he later became a Whig. Earlier in his public career, he had also served in Congress.

For seventeen years, he was the chamber's outspoken conscience. Although in the minority, Adams opposed the Mexican War and fought against the extension of slavery. It was as a congressman in 1841 that Adams argued successfully before the Supreme Court to win freedom for the slave mutineers aboard the Spanish ship *Amistad*.

Which former president presided over a peace conference in 1861 in an attempt to prevent the Civil War?

Abortive Assembly

In February 1861, former President John Tyler chaired a convention of twenty-one states in an endeavor to forestall the outbreak of war. It was ignored by President-Elect Lincoln and the members-designate of his new cabinet.

Who is the only president to be elected to an office of the Confederacy?

Johnny Reb

In November 1861, John Tyler was elected to the Confederate Congress but died suddenly in the Exchange Hotel in Richmond, Virginia, before he actually could take his oath in the chamber in the state capitol of Richmond. Before that he was serving in the provisional Confederate Congress. The North regarded him as a traitor. The U.S. Congress did not erect a memorial to the former president on his grave until 1915.

RELIGION

Four presidents never joined a church. Who were they?

Piety and the Presidency

Thomas Jefferson, Abraham Lincoln, Andrew Jackson, and Rutherford B. Hayes. Hayes, however, was a very devout Christian, was baptized a Presbyterian, and regularly attended the Episcopal church before he married. Hayes then attended his wife's Methodist church. He prayed twice a day but never became a member of a specific church.

Which president wrote out a prayer that he read before his inaugural address?

A Prayerful President

Dwight D. Eisenhower. In part it read:

> Give us, we pray, the power to discern right from wrong and allow all our words and actions to be governed thereby and by the laws of this land. Especially we pray that our concern be for all people, regardless of station, race, or calling . . .

Eisenhower is the only president to begin his inaugural address with a prayer.

Which president was once a licensed minister?

Preacher President

James Garfield was president of the Eclectic Institute at Hiram, Ohio. This was, in part, a religious seminary that prepared ministers for the Disciples of Christ. Although Garfield considered himself only a lay preacher, he was, in fact, qualified to be a minister for that sect.

Which president, while he was general, banished all Jews from Tennessee?

Policy Pogrom?

General Ulysses S. Grant, in his campaign to drive out the Confederate forces from Tennessee, banned all Jews from that state. It was his belief that too many Jewish merchants were engaging in war profiteering in the sale of clothes and food and undermining the efforts of the Union Army.

Which president was so self-conscious about going to church alone that he would have a group of Secret Service men mingle with him so as not to be noted?

Penitent President

John F. Kennedy, as president, was very edgy about going to confession. He would pick some of his fellow Catholics among his Secret Service staff and select different Catholic churches at odd times of the day for saying confession.

Which vice president withdrew from divinity school?

Divinity School Dropout

Vice President Al Gore, the Democratic nominee for president in 2000, dropped out of Vanderbilt School of Religion in 1973. He then attended

Vanderbilt Law School from 1974 to 1976 but did not receive a degree. Afterward, he worked as a journalist for the *Nashville Tennessean*. Vice President Gore, in 2000, won a plurality of the popular vote but lost barely in the electoral college to Texas Governor George W. Bush.

Which president, after he left the White House, became the presidential nominee of the "anti-Catholic" party?

"Know-Nothing" President

Former President Millard Fillmore, in 1856, accepted the presidential nomination from the American Party, which was the anti-Catholic and anti-immigrant party.

The party received the nickname "Know-Nothings" because its members, when asked what were the principles of their party, replied, "I know nothing."

Who was the first president to be married by a Catholic priest?

The President and the Priest

Not John F. Kennedy but Herbert Hoover. Hoover, in 1899, married Lou Henry at the bride's home in Monterey, California. Because there were no Quaker meetings in Monterey, they were married in a civil ceremony by Father Ramon Mestres, a Roman Catholic priest of the San Carlos Borromeo Mission. He was a friend of the Henry family.

Who was the first president to appoint an envoy to the Vatican?

Papal Plenipotentiary

President Harry Truman, in 1950, appointed Myron Taylor to be a special envoy to the Vatican. The Pittsburgh industrialist, who had once headed U.S. Steel, was a Protestant.

Who were the three Unitarian presidents?

Unitarian—Not Trinitarian

John Adams, his son John Quincy Adams, and William Howard Taft. Unitarians do not believe in the divinity of Christ. Jefferson, a Deist, also did not recognize the deity of Christ.

Who are the only two presidents to be "born-again" Christians?

Bipartisan "Born-Agains"

Democrat Jimmy Carter was the first. He owed his victory in the 1976 Iowa caucus partly to help by born-again Christians. It launched his winning campaign.

Then Republican George W. Bush. He was raised an Episcopalian and married a Methodist. He owes his recommitment to Christianity to evangelist Billy Graham and his friend Don Evans, who gave him a Bible with selections for daily reading from passages from the Old and New Testaments and the sayings from Proverbs. His wife's urgings, as well as his bout with alcohol, which he later foreswore, were said to have triggered his refound faith.

Televangelist Pat Robertson, who won the Michigan caucus in the 1988 Republican presidential primary, was a great-grandson of which president?

Pat's Presidential Progenitor

Benjamin Harrison. Robertson, in his losing campaign in 1988, once quoted his great-grandfather in a speech on foreign policy: "America should not be the world's policeman."

In which presidential home was there a ban on Jewish visitors?

House Policy

Harry Truman's. David Susskind, the TV producer, said that in 1953 he would arrive daily at Truman's house at Independence, Missouri, to interview Truman for a future TV special. Susskind would wait on the porch on a cold winter day, while Mrs. Truman went to inform her husband of his arrival. After about the fourth morning, he asked the president in their interview why he was never asked inside.

"You're a Jew, David, and no Jew has ever been in the house."

A nonplussed Susskind replied: "I am amazed that you, who recognized Israel, would say such a thing!"

"David," he explained, "this is not the White House—it's the Wallace house. Bess runs it, and there's never been a Jew inside the house in her or her mother's lifetime."

This has been confirmed by Eddie Jacobs, Truman's former partner in their failed haberdashery business in Kansas City, who said that he was never invited inside the house. Jacobs was one of those who influenced Truman to recognize Israel.

Which first lady was banished from a Quaker meeting?

Denounced Dolley

Dolley Madison. The Society of Friends at Arch Street meeting in Philadelphia, Pennsylvania, had "read" her out of the meeting because she married an Anglican, James Madison. Actually, Dolley Dandridge had been raised an Anglican in Virginia. She had become a Quaker when she married John Todd of Philadelphia. As an Anglican, Dolley could banish the drab Quaker gray garments in her wardrobe and show her true colors.

Who was the first president to attend a Catholic Mass?

Church-Shopper?

Our first president, George Washington. When the Anglican general came to Philadelphia, Pennsylvania, to attend the Continental Congress in 1775, he made a round of various churches—St. Peter's, an Anglican church, the Pine Street Presbyterian Church, a Baptist church, a Lutheran church, and a Friends Meeting at Arch Street. He also attended a Catholic Mass at St. Joseph's Church (now known as Old St. Joseph's). The general was also a politician.

Which president chose as a title for his memoirs a line from the Bible?

"A Time to Heal"

Gerald Ford. He chose the phrase from the passage in Ecclesiastes.

> To everything there is a season, and a time to every purpose under the heaven. A time to be born, and a time to die; a time to plant and a time to reap; a time to kill, and a time to heal.

Ford believed that his administration had healed the wounds of war, Watergate, and a feverish economy.

Who was the first president to appoint a clergyman to the White House staff?

Preacher Pen

Dwight D. Eisenhower appointed Fred Fox, a congregational minister, to assist in speech writing.

Who was the only president to have kissed the ring of the Pope?

Theodore Rex and the Pontifex

Incredibly, it was a Protestant named Theodore Roosevelt. As a boy, the eleven-year-old "Teedie" was taken by his parents on a tour of Europe. On Christmas day, 1869, the boy kissed the ring of Pope Pius IX.

Royalty

Which president was the first to invite the British royal family to spend the night at the White House?

Hot Dog!

Franklin Delano Roosevelt. King George VI and Queen Elizabeth in June 1941 journeyed down by train from Canada. They first stopped at Hyde Park, where the royal couple were treated to their first hot dogs on a picnic. FDR's mother, Sara Delano Roosevelt, was shocked that her son served a picnic lunch outside instead of a formal luncheon in the dining room.

King George pronounced his judgment on the mustard-bunned frankfurter: "Jolly good!" Then they traveled down to Washington and spent a couple of days in the White House.

Who was the first president to invite a monarch to the White House?

Aloha

Ulysses S. Grant. David Kalakaua, the king of the Hawaiian Islands, was received by President Grant in 1887. The king traveled back and forth on American ships—arriving on the USS *Benicia* and returning on the

USS *Pensacola*, traveling around the Cape of Good Horn at the bottom of South America. It was the beginning of the sugar industry in Hawaii, and a reciprocal trade agreement was announced while the king was in Washington, D.C.

Who is the only president to be a godfather to a member of the British royal family?

"Franklin Windsor"?

Franklin Delano Roosevelt. In 1942, the Duke of Kent, the youngest brother of King George VI, served as a proxy for President Roosevelt at the christening of his son, Michael George Charles Franklin. Prince George of Kent's auspicious birth on the Fourth of July 1942 triggered the idea of asking the American president of the United States to be a godfather. The Duke of Kent asked his brother, the king, to call Roosevelt. As an Episcopalian, FDR was an Anglican communicant like the royal family.

Who was the first president to be awarded an honorary knighthood by a British monarch?

Sir Dwight

Dwight D. Eisenhower. For his service in winning the war, General Eisenhower made Knight Grand Cross of the Order of the Bath in 1945. Eisenhower has received more medals than any other American in history.

Which first lady was a ninth-generation descendant of the Indian princess Pocahontas?

Pocahontas Progeny

Edith Bolling Wilson. The second wife of Woodrow Wilson, who was a native Virginian, was proud of her descent from Pocahontas.

Pocahontas, the daughter of Chief Powhatan, married John Rolfe, who took her back to England with him. She was presented to King James I as "Princess Pocahontas" and treated accordingly with the privileges of a princess.

Which president was a king?

The Cornhusker King

Leslie Lynch King Jr. was born in 1913 in Omaha, Nebraska, the son of Leslie Lynch King and Dorothy Ayer Gordon. They divorced in 1915 and the boy took the name of his new stepfather Gerald R. Ford. Ford remembers meeting his blood father only twice—once while he was soda jerking and again after a high school football game. The encounters for young Ford were traumatic.

Bill Clinton is the second president born with a different surname. He was named at birth William Jefferson Blythe IV. His father was killed in an accident before he was born. His stepfather, Roger, adopted Bill, and the name was changed.

Which president was once offered a throne in Europe?

King George?

George Washington. He was offered the crown in the principality of Brunswick in Northern Germany in 1783. (It abuts Hanover, which King George ruled simultaneously with the British Empire.) General Washington turned it down. Washington also rejected a proposal by Colonel Lewis Nicola that he assume a monarchy presiding over the new independent colonies, with the backing of the Continental Army. He said:

With a mixture of great surprise and astonishment, I have read . . . the sentiment. You have submitted . . . such ideas . . . I must view with abhorrence and reprehend with severity.

The granddaughter of which president married a Russian prince?

A Crowning Achievement

Ulysses S. Grant. His granddaughter, Julia, married Russian Prince Michael, a cousin of the czar. For the socially ambitious Mrs. Grant, it was a crowning achievement.

Which first lady developed rheumatism attending the coronation of Napoleon?

La Belle Americane

Elizabeth Kortwright Monroe. When her husband, James Monroe, was minister to France, she attended with him Napoleon's coronation in the Notre Dame cathedral in Paris in a February ceremony in 1796. The six hours in the chilly, dark cathedral triggered a later collapse. Rheumatism set in not long thereafter.

Mrs. Monroe, called "La Belle Americane," however, would not miss the coronation rite. When she became first lady, she was criticized for her social pretensions. She was not reticent in dropping the names of titled elite she had met in her husband's ministries in Britain and France.

Sports

Which president played minor league baseball?

Spray Hitter

Dwight D. Eisenhower was a center fielder in the Kansas League in the summer before he went to West Point. He played under the name of Charlie Wilson because he did not want any professionalism to jeopardize his amateur standing at West Point. His number one priority was to play football there. Eisenhower was a spray hitter with fast legs and defensive skills. Football was his ambition at West Point, but he loved baseball too.

In the White House, he once told some visiting Little Leaguers about two boys emerging from a Kansas swim hole. The blond boy asked the dark-haired lad: "If you could be anything, what do you want to be when you grow up?" The boy said: "President of the United States," and then he in turn questioned the blond youth: "What do you want to be?" And the towheaded youth answered: "Pitcher for the New York Yankees." Then Eisenhower said:

> In America, you can dream of being anything you want. It doesn't matter what color or what religion or how poor you are. That boy who wanted to be president became president all right—president of an Abilene creamery. As for the one who wanted to pitch for the Yankees, he didn't make it either. That was me.

Who was the first president to throw out the opening ball for a baseball season?

Presidential Pitch

William Howard Taft. On April 14, 1910, he threw out the first ball between Clark Griffith's Washington Senators and Connie Mack's Philadelphia A's. Future Hall of Famer Walter Johnson pitched a 3–0 shutout to a crowd of 12,226 that broke all previous attendance records in Washington.

Which president once traded away home-run slugger Sammy Sosa for a song?

Bush League

George W. Bush. The president of the Texas Rangers, in July 1989, traded to the Chicago Cubs the only hitter who would hit more than sixty home runs three times for outfielder Harold Baines, who closed his career in 2001 batting under .200; Sosa still is one of the most feared sluggers in the majors.

Which president stopped legendary football great Jim Thorpe in a game with his tackle?

"Most Promising Halfback"

That was the nickname of Dwight D. Eisenhower who was the star half-back for West Point in his sophomore year at the Academy. The *New York Times* called him "the most promising halfback in the East." A tackle, he became halfback when West Point's star halfback broke his leg. In the next four games, he would score sixteen touchdowns.

In the game with the Carlisle Indians, Ike and a teammate decided to "high-low" the legendary Thorpe. The next play Thorpe looked at Ike and then ran right through him for a touchdown.

Because of an injury to his leg in the next game with Tufts, Eisenhower would never play football again. He was assigned to coach the junior varsity team. His success in that endeavor prompted military authorities to assign Eisenhower to drill recruits before sending them to France. As a result, career soldier Ike never got to see combat in World War I. It was a blow to a professional soldier not to go abroad to France and fight in the biggest war in history up to that time.

Which president was an All-American baseball player in college?

Good Field, No Hit

George H. W. Bush. At Yale, Bush was an All-American in baseball. His position was first base, and his hero was Lou Gehrig—the "Pride of the Yankees." In 1948, the Yale team played Princeton in a game at Yankee Stadium. Bush met a then-dying Babe Ruth. Bush was a slick-fielding first baseman but light with the bat, batting only .289.

Who was the only president to be drafted by the National Football League?

Was There a Ford in Green Bay's Future?

Gerald Ford. A star center at Michigan, Ford played with the 1935 College All-Stars against the Chicago Bears. He was offered a contract by the Detroit Lions and the Green Bay Packers. He also served as line coach for Yale while attending Yale Law School.

Which president was a former baseball announcer?

"Good Afternoon, Cubs Fans . . ."

Ronald "Dutch" Reagan. Reagan broadcast Chicago Cubs games in the 1930s for Des Moines, the powerful outlet for NBC in the Midwest. With only a telegraph receiver feeding him game information, Reagan was good at fleshing out details for the listening audience. Once the receiver went dead, and Reagan had to use his imagination for three innings to keep the game going until the telegraph ticker came back on.

Which president's nickname is derived from an All-American football player's name?

"Win One for the Gipper"

Ronald Reagan. "The Gipper" became his nickname after he played the leading role of Notre Dame's football star George Gipp in the film *Knute Rockne: All-American* with Pat O'Brien. Reagan played the terminally ill football back, beating out John Wayne for the role. In the classic deathbed scene, Reagan tells Pat O'Brien: "Maybe you can ask the boys to go in there and win just once for the Gipper." During the filming, Reagan had to run an eighty-yard touchdown three times before satisfying the director. Afterward, Reagan threw up his lunch.

In his political career, Reagan supporters would often chant, "Win one for the Gipper."

Which presidents have scored a hole in one in golf?

Presidential Perfectos

The first was Richard Nixon—perhaps, one of the least athletic of our modern presidents. He did it before he went to the White House when he was a former vice president at the Bel Air Country Club in Orange County in California in 1961.

Probably the best athlete to serve in the White House in the twentieth century was Gerald Ford although Dwight D. Eisenhower might run a close second.

Ford scored a hole in one three times after he left the presidency, the first during the Danny Thomas Classic in Memphis in 1977. Ford, contrary to the humorous tales of his hitting people with wild shots, was a superlative golfer. A few years later he shot his other two on two different occasions at the Tamarisk Club near Palm Springs.

Eisenhower also made a hole in one in Palm Springs—at the Seven Lake Country Club in 1968. As president, Ike was attacked by Democrats for spending more hours on the golf course than in the Oval Office. Ike befriended golf legend Arnold Palmer, with whom he often partnered in the 1960s.

In 1959, John Hay Whitney, ambassador in London, was asked by Lord Beaverbrook about Senator Kennedy. "Jock, what type of president do you think this young Kennedy will be like?" "Max," Whitney replied, "he'll do for sex what Ike did for golf."

Who was the only president who practiced jujitsu in the White House?

Fitness Fanatic

Theodore Roosevelt. TR was the first president to be a physical fitness advocate. A sickly boy with asthma, he worked hard to develop his body and earned a black belt. In Portsmouth, New Hampshire, for the settlement of the Russian-Japanese war, he charmed the Japanese envoys with his knowledge of jujitsu, which he practiced in the White House basement.

Which president was a champion boxer in college?

Pugilist President

Teddy Roosevelt. At Harvard, Roosevelt was a boxing champion. Once he lost a match when his opponent bloodied his nose after the bell had rung. The audience booed, but Roosevelt stilled them by saying that his combatant had not heard the bell. After that he shook his opponent's hand and the audience cheered.

In the White House, he detached a retina in a match with a sparring partner. He then almost completely lost the sight of that eye.

Who is the only president to have played Little League baseball?

Baseball in His Blood

George W. Bush. He was a catcher with the Midland Cubs in 1960. His coach said of his ability: "He could field but couldn't hit his way out of a paper bag." Bush is a fanatical baseball fan and keeps track of the Texas Rangers' daily scores and listens to some of their games. He said:

> As a boy, I didn't dream of being president. I wanted to be Willie Mays.

Baseball was in his family. His father played baseball for Yale, and his uncle George Walker was part owner of the Mets.

A Hall of Fame pitcher had a correspondence with which president for more than half a century?

A Fast Delivery

Ronald Reagan. In 1936, as a baseball announcer in Iowa, Reagan learned of a sick child in a Des Moines hospital. The lad's hero was strikeout ace Bob Feller of the Cleveland Indians. The fast-balling Feller, who hailed from the cornfields of Iowa, had quite a following in his native state. Reagan wrote to Feller and asked him to write to the stricken youth. Feller immediately wrote back. That was the beginning of a correspondence that would last through the Hollywood years and the Reagan presidency. A hero to many baseball fans, the eighty-two-year-old Feller says today: "Reagan is my number one hero."

Which president was the first to install a billiards table at the White House?

Table Talent

John Adams. The second president learned to love the game while a diplomat in Britain and France. He placed a billiards table on the first floor of the White House in 1800. Adams also enjoyed a game of whist.

Who was the first president to play golf?

Big Bill

William Howard Taft. It was about the only exercise the three-hundred-pound president enjoyed. At the White House, he would play golf at the Burning Tree and Congressional Country Club. For a big man, he was better at small putts than big drives.

STAGE AND SCREEN

Which president's father was a Hollywood film producer?

Movie Mogul

John F. Kennedy. In the late twenties, Joseph Kennedy made more than $5 million as a Hollywood producer as "talkies" began to take hold. At this time, the forty-year-old millionaire began his almost-twenty-year affair with movie star Gloria Swanson.

Which first lady played parts as a film extra in Hollywood?

Small-Town Girl?

Pat Nixon. Patricia Ryan, while going to the University of Southern California, appeared in a few movies. A most noticeable appearance was in *Small-Town Girl* in 1934, a movie that starred Robert Taylor and Janet Gaynor. Mrs. Nixon would later recall that "Robert Taylor was the handsomest man [she] had ever seen."

Later she had a speaking part in *Becky Sharp*, Hollywood's first color movie. Her lines were cut in the final editing. She was once offered a Hollywood contract but turned it down because it was for only one picture.

Pat Ryan was born Thelma Ryan in Ely, Nevada. She was called Pat because she was born near midnight just before St. Patrick's Day in 1912. The Ryans moved to a farm in Los Angeles County when she was a baby.

Which first lady starred in a film entitled Hellcats of the Navy?

Costar!

Nancy Reagan. Under her maiden name, Nancy Davis, she costarred with Ronald Reagan in a movie that came out in 1957. It was the last film they would do together. The "Hellcat" was a navy fighter plane, not a vixenish woman. Nancy Davis gained the notice of Hollywood in 1946 when she appeared in a Broadway play, *Late Song*, with Yul Brynner and Mary Martin. Her greatest role, however, would be her "costarring" role as first lady with her husband Ronald Reagan.

Which president's ex-wife participated in movie's longest kiss?

Smackeroo!

Ronald Reagan. Jane Wyman was Mrs. Reagan in 1941, when she appeared in *You're in the Army Now* with Bud Abbott and Lou Costello, as well as the Andrews Sisters. She was on the receiving end of a three-minute kiss.

Which president had affairs with at least three famous film star beauties?

"Some Like It Hot"

John F. Kennedy. Kennedy, one of the nation's youngest and handsomest presidents, had the glamorous aura of a film star himself. With his father as a former movie producer, Kennedy, as a young man, was no stranger to the Hollywood world. Gene Tierney, Angie Dickinson, and Marilyn Monroe, by published accounts, were three of his women friends.

The most notorious of his relationships was with European film star Inga Arvad. A former Miss Europe, the voluptuous Inga had befriended Hitler before coming to America in 1941 and was under surveillance by the FBI. Judith Exner was also a California bit player in the movies and was lover to Mafia boss Sam Giancana at the same time Kennedy was enjoying her company.

Which president wrote a film script for Hollywood?

Franklin's Film?

Franklin Delano Roosevelt. When Roosevelt was recovering from polio in 1922, the former assistant secretary of the navy wrote a movie script about the USS *Constitution*, nicknamed "Old Ironsides," as the American Navy's most venerable ship. Though he made many revisions, he never succeeded in finding a producer.

Oscar winner Bill Holden served as best man to which president?

Bill Filled the Bill

Ronald Reagan. In his second marriage to Nancy Davis on March 4, 1952, at the Little Brown Church in the San Fernando Valley, Reagan's best friend, Bill Holden, was best man. The Reagans spent the night following the wedding at the Mission Inn in Riverside.

Traditions and Rituals

Who was the first president to officially name the Executive Mansion "the White House"?

White Wash?

Theodore Roosevelt. John Adams called the chief executive's abode "the President's Mansion." (It had been called that in Philadelphia.) Under Jefferson and Madison, it became the Executive Mansion, which would remain its official designation until 1905.

After the White House was burned by the British in 1814, first lady Dolley Madison had it repainted white, and the "White House" became its nickname.

Which president put "In God We Trust" on a coin?

Minted Motto

During his one term in Congress, Abraham Lincoln shared boarding with another Whig lawyer, James Pollock from Pennsylvania. Both voted against the Mexican War, which quickly ended their brief Congressional careers. Pollock was later elected governor of Pennsylvania but was defeated for reelection.

When he was president, Lincoln appointed Pollock to be the director of the mint. In March 1865, Pollcock came to the White House with the idea to put the inscription "In God We Trust" on the nickel. Lincoln agreed and soon signed the executive order.

Which president reintroduced the precedent of delivering personally the State of the Union Address to Congress?

Wilson in Joint Session

Woodrow Wilson, in 1913, reintroduced the tradition last exercised by Thomas Jefferson of delivering the State of the Union Address personally to Congress. Jefferson was much taken with the British practice of the sovereign addressing Parliament. After Jefferson and before Wilson, the State of the Union had been delivered in writing.

Which president personally designed the present presidential seal?

Eagle on a Swivel

Harry Truman. In September 1945, two months after Churchill's defeat as prime minister, President Truman penned a note to Churchill on the bottom of a letter of invitation by the president of Westminster College in Fulton, Missouri: "Come and I'll introduce you."

When the president met Churchill at Union Station in Washington to embark on the private presidential train, *Ferdinand Magellan*, he pointed to the U.S. seal. "I've just redesigned it. The eagle now faces the palm branches and not the arrows."

Thinking of the speech he would deliver the next day, Churchill replied: "With all due respect, Mr. President, I'd like to have the U.S. eagle's neck on a swivel—so it could turn to the olive branch or to the arrows, as the case now demands."

Truman, though he had approved Churchill's talk in advance, denied he had later when a storm erupted over Churchill's warning about the

Soviet Union, America's wartime ally. In fact, Truman telegrammed Joseph Stalin and offered to send the battleship USS *Missouri* to bring him to America and give his side.

He also ordered Dean Acheson not to appear at a dinner honoring Churchill the next week at which Acheson was scheduled to give brief remarks.

Which president chose "The Star-Spangled Banner" as our national anthem?

"O, Say Can You See"

Woodrow Wilson in 1917 signed the executive order making "The Star-Spangled Banner" our national anthem. Some think that Francis Scott Key's martial words make it less fitting than Katherine Lee Bates's "America the Beautiful."

Which president established Thanksgiving Day?

Thanksgiving

Abraham Lincoln, on October 24, 1864, issued an official proclamation for a Thanksgiving observance on the fourth Thursday of November.

In 1789 Washington had issued a proclamation of thanksgiving, but no specific day had been set aside.

"Hail to the Chief" is the signature tune to announce the imminent presence of the president. Which president introduced this White House tradition?

Presidential Prelude

John Tyler. He was the first president to have "Hail to the Chief" played in the White House. The words, from a poem by Sir Walter Scott, are: "Hail to the Chief, who in triumph advances . . ." It was later put to music.

TRANSPORTATION

Which president was sworn in on an airplane?

Oath on Air Force One

Lyndon Johnson took his presidential oath in Air Force One at Love Field, Dallas, on November 22, 1963. The oath was administered by Judge Sarah Tilghman, district judge of Texas. Mrs. Johnson and Mrs. Kennedy and twenty-five others were present.

Who was the first president to ride a train?

Choo-Choo Andy

In June 1833, President Andrew Jackson took a stagecoach from the White House to Ellicott's Mill, Maryland, where he boarded a Baltimore and Ohio train for Baltimore.

Which president was a former officer on a submarine?

The *Sea Wolf*

Annapolis graduate Jimmy Carter attended submarine school in New London, Connecticut. He graduated third in his class. Later he was engineering officer on the first atomic submarine, the *Sea Wolf*.

Who was the first president to have a pilot's license?

Pilot President

Dwight D. Eisenhower. He wanted to sign up for the army flight school at Fort Sam Houston in San Antonio, Texas. For one thing, it was a big hike in a lieutenant's pay, but his fiancée, Mamie Doud, said: "Either the flying machine or Mamie."

Later, as a major in the Philippines (Mamie was back in Seattle where son John was finishing high school), Eisenhower earned his wings.

President Eisenhower and Prime Minister Winston Churchill exchanged mutual congratulations on being the first heads of government to have been pilots. (Churchill earned his license in 1917 while secretary of state for ministries and supplies, as well as Britain's first secretary of air.)

Of course, both President Bushes were pilots—the first in the navy in World War II and the second in the Texas Air National Guard.

Who was the first president to ride in an automobile?

TR and the Electric Car

Theodore Roosevelt rode in the Columbia Electric Victoria in a trip through Hartford, Connecticut. Twenty horse-drawn carriages followed Roosevelt's car in a procession through the city.

Which president was the first to fly in a plane to a national party convention to deliver his acceptance speech?

Flying Franklin

Franklin Delano Roosevelt. Governor Roosevelt, upon hearing news of his nomination for president by the Democratic Convention in Chicago, Illinois, in 1932, chartered a ten-passenger, tri-motor plane and flew from Albany, New York, to Chicago on July 2 to deliver his acceptance speech.

The dramatic flight said more than the speech that followed. Roosevelt was a man who would act fast in meeting the challenge of the Depression.

Who was the first president to fly in an airplane?

Airborne Teddy

Theodore Roosevelt, as a former president, rode in an airplane on October 11, 1910, in St. Louis, Missouri. The pilot was Archie Hoxey.

Who was the first president to have ordered and have custom-built a presidential train?

The *Ferdinand Magellan*

In 1938, President Franklin Delano Roosevelt supervised the building of a special presidential car to be attached to a train. The car was reinforced with steel, a special bulletproof glass, and aisles with rails so that the crippled president could make his way without a wheelchair. It was christened *Ferdinand Magellan.*

Harry Truman would later use it for his vice presidential campaign in 1944. As president, Truman rode in it to take Winston Churchill to Missouri for his Iron Curtain Address in 1946. Two years later, in 1948, that train was the vehicle for Truman's "Give 'em hell folks" campaign across America that won an upset victory.

Who was the first president to drive his own car?

"Big Stick" Shift

Theodore Roosevelt. In 1910, after he left the White House, TR purchased a car and drove it around himself in Oyster Bay, Long Island, the location of his home at Sagamore Hill. Most automobile owners at that time employed chauffeurs.

Which first lady chose the state flower of the state she grew up in as the name for the presidential plane?

Columbine

Mamie Eisenhower chose as the name for the presidential airplane *Columbine*—the blue wildflower that is the state flower of Colorado. Mrs. Eisenhower grew up in Denver. The *Columbine* was the forerunner of Air Force One.

Who was the first president to go down in a submarine?

Down and Under

Theodore Roosevelt in 1905 in New London, Connecticut, not only went down in the submerged submarine but also took over the controls for a while.

VICE PRESIDENTS

One vice president was of minority descent. Who was he?

Chief Republican?

Charles Curtis, the Republican vice president under Herbert Hoover. One-half Kaw Indian, Curtis was born on Indian land in Kansas and was reared on an Indian reservation. He was Senate Republican majority leader in the tenure of Calvin Coolidge. He announced that he would run for president in 1932 but accepted the second spot under Herbert Hoover.

Who was the first vice president to be called "Veep"?

"Servant in the House of the Lord . . ."

Alben Barkley. Harry Truman's vice president was affectionately called "the Veep." The former Senate majority leader who hailed from Kentucky was the last vice president to be born in a log cabin. He became one of the Senate's most formidable orators of his day. To a dispirited Democratic Convention in 1948, he delivered a rousing keynote address. (It was the third time he had been a keynoter to a Democratic Convention.) Truman then picked the fiery orator as his running mate in 1948.

The new vice president was given the nickname "Veep" by his ten-year-old grandson in 1949. That same year the seventy-one-year-old

Barkley married a thirty-eight-year-old widow, Jane Hadley. In 1952, he made a brief run for the presidential nomination and later returned to the Senate in 1955. In 1956, while speaking at Washington and Lee University in Lexington, Virginia, he collapsed and died, just after quoting the Bible saying: "I'd rather be a servant in the house of the Lord than sit in the seats of the mighty." Barkley was the oldest man to serve as vice president.

Which vice president said, "What this country needs is a good five-cent cigar"?

". . . But a Good Cigar Is a Smoke"

Thomas Marshall. This Indiana vice president under Woodrow Wilson uttered this profundity while presiding in the Senate. A droll Hoosier, he also replied when asked about the significance of the vice presidency:

> Once there were two brothers. One ran away to sea. The other was elected vice president, and nothing was ever heard of either of them again.

Which vice presidents who never became president by death were elected later to the presidency?

Veep Victors

John Adams in 1797; Thomas Jefferson in 1801; Martin Van Buren in 1840; Richard Nixon in 1968; and George H. W. Bush in 1988.

Which incumbent vice presidents failed to win the presidential election?

Defeated Veeps

The incumbent Vice President John Breckinridge was defeated in 1860; Vice President Richard Nixon lost in 1960; Vice President Hubert

Humphrey lost in 1968; Vice President Walter Mondale lost in 1980; and Vice President Albert Gore was defeated in 2000.

Who was the only vice president who also had been Speaker of the House?

Bicameral Boss

Schuyler Colfax. Colfax holds the unique distinction of presiding over both houses of Congress in his elective capacity. Congressman Colfax from Indiana had been Speaker of the House for six years, when he was tapped to be Grant's running mate in 1868. As vice president, he was the subject of reports about his involvement in the Credit Mobilier Scandal—the company that constructed the Union Pacific Railroad. Colfax was dumped from the Republican ticket in 1872.

The grandson and namesake of which vice president twice ran for president?

"Madly for Adlai"

Adlai E. Stevenson. The grandfather of Illinois Governor Adlai Stevenson, who twice lost to Eisenhower, served as vice president under Grover Cleveland.

The son of a slave-holding farmer in Kentucky, Stevenson moved to Bloomington, Illinois, where he, in his twenties, was a supporter of Stephen Douglas. He was elected vice president in 1892. Later, in 1900, he ran for vice president with William Jennings Bryan and lost.

Which vice president never served?

God Save [the] King

William King. King was elected vice president as the running mate of Franklin Pierce. A native of Alabama, King served in the Senate from that state for three decades. At the time of his election in 1852, King was suffering from tuberculosis. Following his election, he repaired to Cuba to recover. Too ill to return for the inauguration ceremonies, he took his vice-presidential oath in Havana. Later he returned to his home in Cahaba, Alabama, where he died, never assuming his duties as vice president.

What two vice presidents resigned their office?

Stepping Down

John C. Calhoun in 1832 and Spiro T. Agnew in 1973. Calhoun resigned in December 1832 in protest to President Jackson's opposition to Calhoun's nullification policy of states rights. Agnew was forced to resign in 1973. He had faced charges in a kickback scheme when serving as governor of Maryland.

Two vice presidents represented a different political party than the president under whom they served. Who were they?

Two-Party Government?

Thomas Jefferson and Andrew Johnson. Jefferson lost the presidency to John Adams in 1796 and under the Constitution at the time became vice president. Adams was a Federalist like George Washington, under whom he had served as vice president. Jefferson was head of a new party of anti-Federalists who called themselves Democratic-Republicans, the forerunner of today's Democratic Party.

Andrew Johnson was the Democratic governor of Tennessee. President Abraham Lincoln, in 1864, replaced Vice President Hannibal Hamlin of Maine with Johnson. Lincoln forced his selection on the Republican Convention for reasons of state and diplomatic policy. Britain and France were threatening to recognize the Confederacy. Lincoln told his political lieutenant, Alexander McClure, in Pennsylvania:

The British and French don't know that the number two position in our government is not all that important. Johnson is from the South and his selection proves that this is not a sectional fight but a fight about slavery.

It worked. Britain and France, which were not sympathetic to the institution of slavery, did not recognize the Confederacy.

A city in the fiftieth state is named after which vice president, who served under Theodore Roosevelt?

Alaska Appellation

Charles Fairbanks. Fairbanks was born in a one-room log cabin in Unionville Center, Ohio, in 1852. He developed a successful law practice as a railroad attorney in Indianapolis, Indiana. As senator, he actively campaigned to be vice president in 1904, running with President Theodore Roosevelt. In 1912, Fairbanks supported President Taft against Roosevelt. Then, four years later, he ran with Charles Evans Hughes in his losing race against President Wilson.

The second most populous city in Alaska was named after him when he was vice president in 1905.

Which vice president was tried for treason?

The Burr Conspiracy

Aaron Burr. In 1800, the New York politician was elected vice president with Thomas Jefferson, with whom he broke off relations shortly thereafter. He did not run for vice president in 1804. Instead, he ran for governor of New York, where he was defeated, largely because of Alexander Hamilton. Burr would kill Hamilton in a duel that same year. Indicted for murder, Burr fled New York and tried to separate the southwestern states acquired under the Louisiana Purchase to make himself leader of this new nation. Burr was arrested in 1807 and tried for treason before

Chief Justice Marshall. He was acquitted much to the disappointment of President Thomas Jefferson, who blamed Marshall who was his cousin and political enemy.

Which vice president was a musical composer?

Composer Charles

Charles Dawes. This vice president under Coolidge was a talented musician and composer. His work "Melody in A Major" gained acclaim in 1911. He wrote the popular song "It's All in the Game."

Dawes also won the Nobel Prize for Peace for the Dawes Plan to stabilize the German economy. Dawes did not get along with President Coolidge. Hoover, however, would make him ambassador to Great Britain and later head of the Reconstruction Finance Corporation. He achieved the nickname "Hell and Maria" because after the war, in answer to a question of overpayment to a Senate committee, he captured America's attention with an expletive: "Sure we paid. We didn't dicker. 'Hell and Maria,' we weren't trying to keep a set of books—we were trying to win a war."

Which city in Texas is named after a vice president?

The Big "D"

Dallas. George Mifflin Dallas, the vice president under James Polk, came from a distinguished Philadelphia family. His father, Alexander, had been secretary of treasury, appointed by James Madison. Dallas served as mayor of Philadelphia, senator, and U.S. minister to Russia. As vice president, Dallas broke the tie on a vote that lowered the tariff rates. The action pleased the South but so angered eastern manufacturers that Dallas had to move his family out of Philadelphia.

The annexation of Texas by President Polk caused the citizens of a little community on the Trinity River to take the name of Polk's vice president.

Which two vice presidents served under two different presidents?

Split Service

George Clinton served under Thomas Jefferson from 1805 to 1809. Jefferson had broken with Aaron Burr, the vice president, in his first term. Clinton would also be vice president under James Madison. The New Yorker had originally fought strenuously against the ratification of the U.S. Constitution.

John Calhoun, a South Carolinian, first served as vice president under John Quincy Adams from 1825 to 1829. He then was elected as vice president with Andrew Jackson.

Which vice president's wife was African American?

Slave Lover?

Richard Mentor Johnson. This Kentuckian, who was the ninth vice president, earned widespread fame as the soldier who actually killed Tecumseh, the famous Indian chief in the Indiana Territory. At that time, Colonel Johnson commanded a regiment under General William Henry Harrison. In Congress, he was a spirited advocate of Andrew Jackson. For that loyalty, President Jackson dictated to his successor, Martin Van Buren, that Johnson be his vice president.

Johnson took a slave as his common-law wife and sent their mulatto children to school. For this, he was reviled in the South and not renominated for vice president in 1840.

WHAT
OTHERS SAID

The father of one president told his son: "If you were a girl, you'd be in a family way all the time. You can't say no." Who was the president?

Soft Touch

Warren G. Harding. George Harding said this of his easygoing and accommodating son. The Harding administration found itself awash in scandals. The root cause of these reeking deals was the influence-peddling cronies of Harding. Harding couldn't say no to his friends.

Thomas Jefferson said of one president: "He is one of the most unfit men I know for such a place." Who was the president?

"E Pluribus Unum"

Andrew Jackson. Jefferson and Jackson are considered the two founders of today's Democratic Party. Yet the patrician Thomas Jefferson, who championed the common man, had little use for Andrew Jackson, a real man of the people, who rose to be a general and was talked of as a potential president. In his waning years, Jefferson made this characterization of Jackson.

President Jackson was once given an honorary degree at Harvard, much to the horror of Harvard graduate John Quincy Adams. When the degree was read in Latin to the unlettered Jackson, he was asked by a member of the crowd in attendance: "Give us a little Latin, Andy."

Jackson reportedly answered: "E pluribus unum, the sine qua non." The nationalist Jackson knew at least two Latin phrases—the first means one [nation] out of many [states], and the other describes an essential requirement.

Benjamin Franklin said these words about a president: "Honest, intelligent, and sometimes out of his mind." Who was the president?

Honest to a Fault

John Adams. Ben Franklin respected Adams, but their personalities clashed. Franklin was genial in personality, discreet in his utterances, and deft in political maneuverings—all qualities that make for success in politics and diplomacy. Adams was irascible, honest to a fault, and clumsy in politics.

They both served in the Continental Congress, and both were appointed peace commissioners in Paris to negotiate the end of the war with Britain.

Which president did Charles Dickens make this comment about: "He looked somewhat worn and anxious, and well he might be, being at war with everybody"?

The Dickens, You Say

John Tyler. The British novelist met Tyler at the White House during his first trip to America. His reactions to his host country in *American Notes* were generally harsh. Nevertheless, he was relatively impressed with Tyler, who was at that time sparring with Mexico and with those who disapproved of his expansionist sentiments in the Southwest.

A president's daughter said this about another president: "He looked like he was weaned on a pickle." Who was the president she was describing?

Pickle Puss?

Calvin Coolidge. Alice Roosevelt Longworth, the tart-tongued daughter of Teddy Roosevelt, so described the pinched-faced Republican president, who could be as "pinch-penny" in his federal budgets.

When he was asked by a reporter if the United States should not forgive the loans to European countries after World War I, the reticent president replied: "They hired the money, didn't they?"

A famous supreme court justice gave his impression of one president: "First-class temperament and second-class mind." Who was the president?

"A Very Pleasant Man"

Franklin Delano Roosevelt. Oliver Wendell Holmes made this comment to his former law clerk, Thomas (Tommy the Cork) Corcoran. In March 1933, the new president paid a visit to the ninety-three-year-old justice.

Roosevelt entered the justice's home off Lafayette Square and asked: "What are you doing, Mr. Justice?" Holmes replied: "Reading Greek."

"Why would anyone do that on this sunny day?" asked FDR.

"To improve my mind, Mr. President."

"Mr. Justice," asked Roosevelt, "you have lived over half the life of this great republic. What advice do you give to this new president?"

"Mr. President," replied Holmes, "we are in warlike crisis. Marshal your battalions and fight."

Afterward, Corcoran, who would later become one of the New Deal's "brain trust," asked what Holmes thought of the president.

"First-class temperament and second-class mind."

A year before, the respected journalist Walter Lippmann had written of FDR: "He is a pleasant man who, without any important qualifications for the office, would very much like to be president."

Lyndon Johnson said of another president: "He played too much football with his helmet off." Who was the president?

Sacking the Quarterback?

Gerald Ford. LBJ's comment notwithstanding, Ford was hardly stupid. If he had been, he would not have been selected as leader of House Republicans or picked by Nixon as a vice president. Indeed, President Johnson selected him for the Warren Commission on the Kennedy assassination. Ford had riled LBJ when he led a movement to sack Justice Abe Fortas, an old Johnson adviser, in an impeachment attempt.

John Calhoun said of one president: "He is not the race of a lion or of the tiger; he belongs to a lower order—the fox." Who was the president?

Vulpine Van

Martin Van Buren. John Calhoun detested Andrew Jackson but had begrudging respect for Jackson's chief lieutenant, Martin Van Buren. Compared to Jackson, Van Buren's movements were more sly and backhanded.

John Adams said this of the prospects of one man for the White House: "He is too illiterate, unread, and unlearned for his station." Who was the president?

General Knowledge

George Washington. The assessment of Washington by the man who would be his successor as president years later is not without a twinge of envy. General Washington, unlike Adams, was no intellectual, but his gift for leadership far exceeded that of Adams.

A president said this of a later president: "I cannot spare this man. He fights." Who were the two presidents?

Forward Pass

Abraham Lincoln and Ulysses S. Grant. Abraham Lincoln, Grant's commander in chief, made the comment. Lincoln was frustrated by most of his generals' reluctance to commit troops to action in the Civil War. The foremost target of this criticism was General George McClellan. McClellan's delay in advancing the Army of the Potomac toward Richmond exasperated the president.

One day, someone called on Lincoln and stated he had a family problem. His sick relative was in Richmond, and he asked for a pass that would take him behind the lines.

Lincoln asked: "Are you going to really use the pass?"

"Of course, Mr. President."

"Because I gave George McClellan 125,000 'passes' to Richmond, and he still hasn't used them."

A British prime minister said of one president: "Meeting him is like opening your first bottle of champagne." Who was the president?

Effervescent

Franklin Delano Roosevelt. This was Winston Churchill's description of FDR. The two World War II leaders developed a close and intimate rela-

tionship. They came from a similar upper-class background of wealth and privilege. They even shared a common forebear—a great-great-great-great-grandfather. Churchill, while a guest at the White House and Hyde Park, enjoyed the full benefit of the Roosevelt charm, which included FDR's sense of humor, his gift as a raconteur, and his talent for mimicry.

When Roosevelt died in April 1945, weeks before the defeat of Germany, Churchill wrote: "He died on the wings of victory, but he saw them and heard them beating."

Which president was described this way by a cabinet secretary: "He has all the vision of one whose formative years were spent on the south side of a mule"?

Ass-inine?

Harry Truman. Harold Ickes, FDR's secretary of commerce, detested Roosevelt's successor in the same manner that some of President Kennedy's lieutenants hated LBJ. Ickes was opposed to Truman's postwar foreign policy moves. The statement was referring to Truman's rural and provincial upbringing in Missouri.

A former White House adviser had this to say of one president: "He is the biggest bigot I have ever known." Who was the president?

"Darkie" Stories!

Woodrow Wilson. Colonel Frank House, Wilson's closest adviser, was appalled at Wilson's attitude toward African Americans. Wilson was a native Virginian whose formative years were spent in the South. A staunch believer in segregation, he segregated the military barracks and restroom accommodations in the District of Columbia. Wilson's telling of "darkie" stories about "Rastus" or "Moses" in shuffling dialect to amuse his guests offended House.

A secretary of state said of one president: "A meeting with him is like being in a bathtub of ink." Who was the president?

Hair-Splitting Hoover

Herbert Hoover. His secretary of state, Henry Stimson, who later served Franklin Roosevelt as secretary of war, found his dealings with Hoover onerous. In comparison to Roosevelt, who was interested in the grand concepts and bored with detail, Hoover was the opposite. The former engineer would drag out meetings with nit-picking demands for statistics and details.

Thomas Paine said this of a president: "His character is sort of a nondescribable, chameleon-colored thing called prudence. It is in many cases a substitute for principle." Who was the president?

Principles or Prudence?

George Washington. Thomas Paine, the writer of *Common Sense*, once adored Washington and castigated "the sunshine patriots" who didn't remain in the field and help the general fight. A radical who supported the French Revolution, Paine became disillusioned with President Washington, who would not ally the United States with France in its war against England.

Franklin Delano Roosevelt wrote this about a future president: "He certainly is a wonder, and I wish we could make him president of the United States. There could not be a better one." Who was the president?

"Sic Transit Gloria"

Herbert Hoover. Franklin Delano Roosevelt said this in 1919 about the man he would defeat in 1932. Hoover was at that time revered in the world as the feeder of the hungry in Europe. This self-made millionaire, who now had turned his abilities to serving mankind, was considered in the twenties an embodiment of the American dream. The Depression would destroy that image.

President William Henry Harrison, as a congressman, once wrote this of a president who was his predecessor: "He is a disgusting man to do business with—coarse, dirty, and clowning in his address and stiff and abstracted in his opinions." Who was the president?

Dirty and Dry?

John Quincy Adams. General Harrison was a soldier who prided himself on his dress and appearance. Adams did not. In his personal relations, Adams could be witty and jocular. It was a contrast to his speeches, which were often dry and bookish.

Abraham Lincoln made this comment about a president: "He is a bewildered, confounded, and miserably perplexed man." Who was the president?

Perplexed, Bothered, and Bewildered

James K. Polk. Whig Congressman Abraham Lincoln was an opponent of Polk and thought that Polk was wrong entering the United States in the war against Mexico. Polk was deeply religious, and Lincoln suspected the president, in his heart, knew the war was unjust.

Theodore Roosevelt made this observation about a preceding president: "He is a cold-blooded, narrow-minded, prejudiced, obstinate, timid, old-psalm-singing Methodist politician." Who was the president?

Lip Service?

Benjamin Harrison. Theodore Roosevelt had campaigned for Harrison in the Midwest in 1888, and Harrison appointed him a civil service commissioner in 1889. Yet Harrison, who in his presidential campaign supported the practice of merit-based government service, did little to put those principles in play.

Which president said to Franklin Delano Roosevelt: "My little man. I am making a strange wish for you. It is that you will never be a president of the United States."

Wishful Thinking

Grover Cleveland. At the age of five, Roosevelt was taken in 1887 to the White House, where he was introduced to the president. The Hyde Park Roosevelts were Democrats. A weary president patted Roosevelt on the head and pronounced his wish.

Mark Twain gave this high praise to one president: "Your patriotic virtues have won you the homage of half the nation and enmity of the other half. This places you upon a summit as high as Washington's." Who was the president?

"Rock"

Grover Cleveland. Mark Twain, a nominal Republican, held politicians in minimal esteem ("the only native criminal class"). Yet he admired Grover Cleveland, a Democrat, for his rocklike integrity and adherence to principles. "The verdict for you is rock and will stand," said Twain of him.

President Truman described a nineteenth-century president this way: "He was the best looking president the White House ever had, but he ranked with Buchanan and Coolidge as one of the worst." Who was the president?

"Handsome Is as Handsome Does"

Franklin Pierce. Harry Truman was a keen student of American history. He had great admiration for Polk but little for Pierce. Certainly Pierce ranks with Harding as one of the more handsome presidents. If Pierce had a certain style about him, his administration lacked substance of achievement. His principle act of legislation was the Kansas-Nebraska Act, which triggered a bloody conflict between proslavery and antislavery factions. Pierce was so unpopular that he was denied renomination by his own party.

John Quincy Adams described one president in these words: "He is a barbarian who could not write a sentence of grammar and can hardly write his own name." Who was the president?

Backwoods Boor?

Andrew Jackson. His predecessor, John Quincy Adams, did not attend Jackson's inauguration. Adams also boycotted the ceremonies of his college, Harvard, when his cousin Josiah Quincy, the college president, gave the barely educated Andrew Jackson an honorary degree.

John Quincy Adams and Andrew Jackson were virtual opposites—one a Northern antislavery Whig and a scholar and the other a Southern proslavery Democrat who preferred racing horses and raising gamecocks to reading books.

Robert F. Kennedy said this of a president: "He tells so many lies that he convinces himself after a while that he's telling the truth. He just doesn't recognize the truth or a falsehood." Who was the president?

A Brother's Bile

Lyndon Johnson. Robert Kennedy was appalled when his brother John selected Senator Johnson to be his running mate in 1960. It was a shrewd move by JFK. It helped him carry most of the South, including Texas, without which Kennedy would have surely lost. Robert Kennedy despised the man who succeeded his brother at the White House, and the feeling was mutual.

One president's daughter said of another president: "He is not a bad man—just a slob." Who was the president she was talking about?

Sloppy and Slovenly

Warren G. Harding. The acerbic Alice Roosevelt Longworth had this character summation of Harding. The word "slob" is usually associated with looks and appearance, but it was Harding's choice of cronies and his negligence in administration that was morally sloppy and slovenly.

Fidel Castro had this observation of a president: "He is the biggest liar of all American presidents—the worst terrorist in the history of mankind—a madman, an imbecile, and a bum." Who was the president?

A Communist Commendation?

Ronald Reagan. If hatred by your enemies is a form of praise, Reagan should be pleased by this bit of vitriol by Fidel Castro. Reagan earned the hatred of every Communist when he made an address in 1982 that saluted freedom and predicted that "Marxism is on the ash heap of history."

WOULD YOU BELIEVE?

Which president killed a man?

Avenging Andy

"Harlot," "whore," "strumpet." These were some of the epithets hurled at Rachel Donelson Jackson. Rachel never became first lady; she died of a heart attack in November 1828, following a nervous breakdown after her husband, Andrew Jackson, had been elected but before he entered the White House. In Jackson's mind, the rumors that chased her all her life about the circumstances surrounding her first marriage finally broke her heart.

"Bigamist" was one of the names she was called, and technically it had been true. She had married a Captain Lewis Robards in 1785. In 1790, the legislature of Virginia granted her the right to sue for divorce—a grant that she mistakenly assumed was a divorce. She married Jackson in 1791. When they learned that the divorce proceedings had not been completed, Rachel gained her divorce and remarried Jackson in 1793.

Jackson was the kind of man who attracted the fierce loyalty of friends and the hatred of foes. One of his political enemies who had bruited gossip about Rachel was Charles Dickinson. The hotheaded Jackson challenged him to a duel and shot to kill. In his 1828 campaign for the presidency, the rumors surfaced again. Mrs. Jackson died shortly after Jackson won, and Jackson blamed the malicious gossip.

Because of the toll that the social slights had taken on his wife, President Jackson was furious when many of his cabinet members snubbed Peggy O'Neil Eaton, the former tavern proprietress who married John Eaton, his secretary of war. The result was that Jackson leaned not on his cabinet for advice, but on the "kitchen cabinet," a group of friends and advisers.

Which president as a parlor trick would write a Greek sentence with his right hand, write a Latin sentence with his left, and speak German at the same time?

The Garfield Gambit

James Garfield, who was a classics scholar at Williams College, was proficient in Greek and Latin. He had picked up German in the docks of Lake Erie working as a canal boy. Later as a politician, he would address his German constituents in their native tongue.

As a parlor trick he would entertain his grandchildren or others by writing Greek with his right hand, writing Latin with his left hand, and speaking phrases in German at the same time. His family thought Garfield was born left-handed but had been taught to write with his right hand.

Which president broke his arm jumping out of a window to escape being caught by the husband of the woman with whom he was trysting?

Peccadillo in Paris

When the forty-two-year-old Thomas Jefferson arrived in France in 1785 to be minister to France, Count Vergennes, the French prime minister, asked Jefferson: "Monsieur, have you come to replace Dr. Franklin?" Jefferson answered: "Monsieur Le Comte, no one could ever replace Dr.

Franklin. I am only succeeding him." Benjamin Franklin had been a living legend. Not the least of the assets of his popularity was his appeal to the opposite sex.

Jefferson, though he was passably conversational in French, did not, like Franklin, make an effort to mix with French society.

Jefferson was less gregarious than Franklin, and most of his friends belonged to an English-speaking set in Paris. Jefferson, however, like Franklin, did engage in a few liaisons. One was with a Londoner's wife, the beautiful Mrs. Cosway. One day, the husband arrived home unexpectedly. In his haste to escape, Jefferson jumped out of the window, breaking his arm. He was never able to play the violin again. Jefferson said later that he fractured it trying to jump over a fence.

Which president hanged a man in official duty?

He Got the Hang of It!

As sheriff of Erie County, New York, Grover Cleveland did not delegate the macabre duty of hanging condemned criminals. He did it himself. Cleveland carried out the sentence three times in his tenure. The *Buffalo Express* on September 7, 1872, reported that "Sheriff Cleveland stood at the gallows with his right hand on the rod attached to the trap bolt, and at fourteen minutes past twelve, Mr. Emerick gave the signal."

The daughter of which president married a man who was also to become an American president?

Captain Jeff

General Zachary Taylor, "Old Rough and Ready," was a stern father. His daughters were prohibited from dating the officers under his command. Yet daughter Sarah—against her father's wishes—eloped with Captain Jefferson Davis in 1835. She would die three months later.

Davis would serve under his former father-in-law in the Mexican War. Later he became a United States senator from Mississippi. He resigned in 1861 and was elected president of the Confederacy. He was, if not a U.S. president, an American president.

The son of which president was at the scene of three presidential assassinations?

Presidential Jinx

Abraham Lincoln. Poor Robert Lincoln! It was not enough for him to have suffered through his father's assassination in Washington when he was home from Harvard. He had to relive his father's death two more times. First, as secretary of war, he went to the Washington railroad station to see off President Garfield on July 2, 1881, when the chief executive was shot. Then again Robert Lincoln received an invitation to meet

President William McKinley at the Pan American Expedition in Buffalo on September 6, 1901, when a gunman shot and killed the president.

Thereafter Robert Lincoln refused all invitations to meet or see presidents.

Which president fathered an illegitimate child while senator a year before he ran for the White House?

Wanton Warren

Warren G. Harding was one of our more handsome presidents. With the face of a matinee idol, Harding had a libido that exceeded his ambition. His philandering was endured by his wife, who was five years older than he was. She was the daughter of his hometown's richest banker and was called "the Duchess" for her imperious ways. If Harding had a wandering eye, he never had to wander far. Women adored him. One buxom blonde who did catch President Harding's attention when he was senator was Nan Britton, who was thirty years younger than the fiftyish Harding. She bore him a daughter named Elizabeth.

One time, when the president was in a naked embrace with Nan, the Secret Service general knocked on the door and whispered: "The Duchess is coming." The guard held the gate as Harding dressed and Nan departed.

Which incumbent president offered to run as vice president with a popular general if the military hero agreed to run for president?

Harry's Offer

The landslide victory of a Republican Congress in 1946 made President Truman doubtful of his chances to win the 1948 presidential election. The most popular hero in America was General Eisenhower—known as "Ike." The Democrats had held the White House for sixteen years since Franklin Delano Roosevelt's election in 1932, and the nation was ripe for a change. After the patrician Franklin Delano Roosevelt, Harry Truman seemed to lack the majesty and stature to be president. On the other hand, Eisenhower, who had led the biggest army in history to victory, had all the qualifications. President Truman, in 1947, took Army Chief of Staff Eisenhower aside and offered him the Democratic nomination for president in 1948 and said that he would run as vice president. Eisenhower declined.

Which president fathered an illegitimate child whose mother was a sister of his wife?

Dally with Sally

Sally Hemings was the mulatto half-sister of Martha Skelton Jefferson. She was also Mrs. Jefferson's personal maid. When Martha Jefferson died at age thirty-three in 1782, it is presumed the relationship between Jefferson and his wife's in-house servant ripened. DNA studies confirm the Jefferson genes in the Hemings's descendants.

The son of which president was rescued from a train pit by a man whose brother would kill this same president weeks later?

Did Booth Save Lincoln's Life?

Abraham Lincoln. In March 1865, Robert Lincoln was switching trains in Passaic, New Jersey. He was a Harvard student coming down from Boston. While he was making his way—bag in hand—across the platform to board a train for Washington, he tripped over his bag and fell into a railway pit.

A broad-shouldered man, seeing the plight of the young passenger who was trapped in the path of oncoming trains, reached down and pulled him to safety.

The twenty-year-old looked at his rescuer's face and immediately recognized him.

"You're Edwin Booth, the actor," he said.

"Yes," was the reply. "I'm headed for Philadelphia, where I'm playing Hamlet."

"My father," said the student, "is a great admirer of yours. I'd like to have your autograph. My name is Robert Lincoln."

"Are you any relation to the president?" asked Booth.

"I'm his son," was the answer.

"Well, tell your father that I'm a great admirer of his."

Weeks later, Edwin's younger brother John would kill Robert Lincoln's father.

Which president died with no money in his pocket except for five Confederate dollars?

Pocket Change

Abraham Lincoln. The stricken Lincoln, after he was shot, was carried from Ford's Theater across the street to the Peterson rooming house and later taken to the second floor. The unconscious president was undressed and put on a bed. The only money in his pocket were five Confederate dollars. It was because he had visited Richmond, Virginia, the week before and collected them as souvenirs.

Curiously, weeks before, John Wilkes Booth, the assassin, had visited the Peterson rooming house to see a fellow actor who was lodging there—in the same room in which Lincoln would die. In fact, Booth had taken a nap on what would be the Lincoln deathbed weeks later.

Which president was shot during a campaign speech for the presidency and yet continued speaking?

"Strong as a Bull Moose"

Theodore Roosevelt was shot leaving the Hotel Gilpatrick in Milwaukee on October 14, 1912. He was on his way to an auditorium to deliver a speech in the presidential campaign of that year when he was shot in the chest. The would-be assassin was opposed to Roosevelt's bid to win a third term. Roosevelt was running as the Progressive Party nominee. It was nicknamed the Bull Moose Party because Roosevelt had said: "I'm as strong as a bull moose."

Although the bullet pierced his chest making his shirt bloody red, Roosevelt told his audience that "there's a bullet in this body," and he went on to speak for fifty minutes. Edwin Shrank, the gunman, was committed to a mental hospital. When Roosevelt died in 1919, Shrank was quoted as saying: "Roosevelt was a good man and a good president." Shrank had been a Milwaukee bartender.

Which president was taught to read and write by his wife?

"Teach Me Tonight"

Of all the first ladies, Eliza McCordle Johnson was the youngest when she married. In Greeneville, Tennessee, at age fifteen, she wed Andrew Johnson, who was two years her senior. Johnson, who never attended any school, was illiterate. He could write his name but little more. In the evenings, after he worked all day as a tailor, his wife taught him to read and write. Without his wife, he never would have entered a political career, rising from mayor to governor and then vice president and president.

Which president was confirmed by the Senate for his appointment to the Supreme Court but turned it down?

Justice Denied

John Quincy Adams was appointed by President Madison in 1810 and was then confirmed by the Senate. Adams, however, was serving in St. Petersburg as minister to Russia. The letters announcing his appointment and later his confirmation took weeks to reach him. When he learned about his appointment, he wrote back to refuse it.

Adams entertained ambitions to be president, like his father; and the Court appointment would have precluded that.

Which president was sworn in by his own father?

Calvin and the Colonel

Vice President Calvin Coolidge was vacationing in Vermont when he heard the news of President Harding's death in San Francisco. Harding was returning from a trip to Alaska.

At 2:47 A.M. Colonel John Coolidge, a notary public and justice of the peace, swore in his own son at the Coolidge homestead by the light of a kerosene lamp—with only five present. Justice Coolidge was a colonel in the Vermont state militia.

BIBLIOGRAPHY

Ambrose, Stephen. *Eisenhower: Soldier and President*. New York: Touchstone Books, 1991.

Anthony, Carl Sferrazza. *First Ladies*. New York: Quill, William Morrow, 1990.

Baker, Jean. *James Buchanan*. New York: Times Books, Henry Holt and Co., 1998.

Caroli, Betty Boyd. *First Ladies*. New York: Oxford University Press, 1987.

DeGregorio, William A. *The Complete Book of U.S. Presidents*. New York: Gramercy Books, 2001.

Kane, Joseph Nathan. *Presidential Fact Book*. New York: Random House, 1998.

Karabell, Zachary. *Chester A. Arthur*. New York: Times Books, Henry Holt and Co., 1999.

McCullough, David. *John Adams*. New York: Simon & Schuster, 2001.

Morris, Edmund. *Rise of Theodore Roosevelt*. New York: Modern Library, 2001.

———. *Theodore Rex*. New York: Random House, 2001.

Neal, Steve. *The Eisenhowers: Reluctant Dynasty*. New York: Doubleday & Co., 1967.

Neely, Mark, ed. *The Abraham Lincoln Encyclopedia*. New York: McGraw-Hill, 1982.

Nixon, Richard Milhous. *Richard Nixon Memoirs*. New York: Grosset & Dunlap, 1978.

Pitch, Anthony. *Exclusively First Ladies Trivia*. Washington, D.C.: Mino Publishing, 1985.

Siegenthaler, John. *James K. Polk*. New York: Times Books, Henry Holt and Co., 2000.

Smith, Bernie. *The Joy of Trivia*. New York: Bell Publishing, 1976.

Smith, Richard Norton. *An Uncommon Man*. New York: High Plains Publishing, 1984.

Trefousse, Hans. *Rutherford Hayes*. New York: Times Books, Henry Holt and Co., 2000.

Wallechinsky, David, and Irving Wallace. *The People's Almanac*. New York: Doubleday, 1975.

Widmer, Ted. *Martin Van Buren*. New York: Times Books, Henry Holt and Co., 2000.

Wills, Garry. *James Madison*. New York: Times Books, Henry Holt and Co., 2002.

INDEX